The Easy Way
Discourses

_____

By Harold Klemp

ECKANKAR
Minneapolis
www.Eckankar.org

The Easy Way Discourses

Visit our Web site at www.Eckankar.org.

Text illustrations by Signy Cohen, Claude Gruffy, Rebecca Lorio, Fraser MacDonald, Valerie Taglieri, Nick Vlcek, Ron Wennekes, and Betsy White

MAHANTA

These discourses have been authored by and published under the supervision of the Mahanta, the Living ECK Master, Sri Harold Klemp. They are the Word of ECK. These discourses are your private and confidential study of the ECK teachings. They are for your own spiritual benefit and may be shared only with those in your immediate household or ECK Satsang class.

Contents

Introduction

Pay close attention to the gentle rhythm in
The Easy Way Discourses, *for it carries the
secret melody of divine love, wisdom, and
understanding.* (p. 1)

Welcome to *The Easy Way Discourses*!

As you read each lesson, you will find a special spiritual exercise for the month as well as workbook activities to enhance your understanding of *The Easy Way Discourses*. The workbook activities can help you:

- become more aware of how the Mahanta, the Living ECK Master works with you one-on-one through the ECK discourses to open your heart to the secret teachings of ECK;

- recognize the spiritual experiences you're having throughout this year of study.

How to Get the Most Out of Your Discourse Study

- Study just one lesson per month.

- The first day of study, get an overview by reading the entire lesson. You can underline or highlight important sentences and make notes in the margin if you like.

- Watch for your special gift: the spiritual exercise given

at the end of the lesson. Daily practice of the Spiritual Exercises of ECK is your key to truth and spiritual freedom.

- Look over the workbook activities for the month's lesson. Do them at your own pace throughout the month.

- The second day of study, slow down and read only a paragraph or two of the lesson before bedtime, and contemplate on that. Proceed this way until you have covered the entire lesson.

- At the end of the month, you can review the lesson. For more helpful information, see chapter 2, "ECK Discourse Study Tips," and chapter 3, "Tips for Spiritual Exercises and Dream Study," in *Welcome to the Wonderful World of ECK! Your Membership Guidebook.*

Overview and Tips for Workbook Activities

- Workbook activities begin with the "Welcome" letter. They serve as a guide and supplement to your study of each month's discourse lesson.

- The last section of workbook activities, based on the "What's Next" letter, can help you chart a course for your next year of ECK study.

- The ✎ icon shows where you can write your responses to an activity. Extra writing pages are provided in case you need more space.

- You will find specially selected audio excerpts from some of the Master's talks on the enclosed CD. The 🎧 icon lets you know when to pause and listen to these excerpts, which include experiences, insights, or spiritual exercises relevant to the subject of the lesson. For a listing of the complete seminar talks and the corresponding chapters of the Mahanta Transcripts series of books where they are in print, see "Recordings and Mahanta Transcripts" on pages 245–47.

Satsang Classes

If you wish, you can also join an ECK Satsang class where members of ECKANKAR meet for spiritual study, led by a trained ECK teacher (Arahata).

Satsang is a wonderful opportunity to discuss the discourse and share experiences, insights, and questions. See chapter 4, "ECK Satsang Classes (Discourse Study)" in *Welcome to the Wonderful World of ECK! Your Membership Guidebook* for how to find classes in your area and for more information.

Sri Harold Klemp
The Mahanta, the Living ECK Master

Welcome

Dear Friend in ECK,

Welcome to the secret worlds of God.

In the coming year, you can test and weigh the teachings of ECK in the scales of truth. Thousands like you have already done so, and now here's your own chance to try.

The standard by which to judge truth is spiritual freedom. Make that standard your own and never turn your back on it. Odd as it may sound, many people do.

You have joined a spiritual community of people who share the desire for truth—a divine principle to help them in every detail of life. Many of the ideas you will discover in ECK do challenge the spirit of inquiry, yet the outer and inner teachings of ECK show the way to profit spiritually from that inquiry.

The Spiritual Exercises of ECK are your key to truth and spiritual freedom. You'll find one in each of the twelve discourses.

Pay close attention to the gentle rhythm in *The Easy Way Discourses*, for it carries the secret melody of divine love, wisdom, and understanding. God is love. There is no higher truth than that. However, few people ever find it because of a fear of giving up old

1

ideas and habits, even though they are the cause of most misery and anxiety in life.

A new world awaits you. Be willing to put a little time, effort, and a lot of heart into the ECK teachings. That is the only way to gain a rich appreciation of the hidden life of Divine Spirit.

You are now ready to start on the road to spiritual freedom.

With spiritual blessings,

Harold Klemp

PS Please study only one lesson per month.* These discourses are written with a secret, internal rhythm that gradually unfolds the consciousness of the student in a very precise and orderly manner.

---

*You will be asked to read a chapter from Stranger by the River while studying lesson 6 of this discourse series. You may wish to obtain a copy of this book beforehand.

Workbook Activities

1.   *Welcome to the secret worlds of God. . . .*
        Pay close attention to the gentle rhythm in The
        Easy Way Discourses, *for it carries the secret*
        melody of divine love, wisdom, and understanding.
        (p. 1)

Ready to begin? Take a few minutes to read the
"Welcome" letter on pages 1–2. Certain words or
phrases may hold special interest or light up for
you. You can highlight these with a marker or
underline them.

2.   *The Spiritual Exercises of ECK are your key to*
        truth and spiritual freedom. . . .
        A new world awaits you. Be willing to put a
        little time, effort, and a lot of heart into the ECK
        teachings. (pp. 1–2)

Prepare to enter this new world of truth and
spiritual freedom. The daily spiritual exercises are
your key.

Look for twenty minutes in your day when you
can really enjoy this gift of experiencing God's
love. What time would work best for you?

3.   *God is love. There is no higher truth than that.* (p. 1)

🎧 Audio Excerpt 1

This discourse series includes a CD with excerpts from ECK seminar talks. The first excerpt, from "The Right of Choice," offers some benefits of doing the Spiritual Exercises of ECK.

Here's a spiritual exercise you can try every day this month:

> With eyes open or closed, take a few deep breaths to relax. Fill your heart, mind, and body with warm love.
> Then begin to sing *HU* in a long, drawn-out sound. Take another breath, and sing *HU* again. Continue for up to twenty minutes (or for as long as you can, even if only for a few minutes).

When you do the Spiritual Exercises of ECK, be open to any way that divine love may come to you, no matter how subtle or fleeting.

What's one benefit—one change for the better— that you've gained from this spiritual exercise?

✑

Spotlight on ECK (Holy Spirit):
Noticing and Remembering the Spiritual Gifts

4. *You have joined a spiritual community of people who share the desire for truth—a divine principle to help them in every detail of life.* (p. 1)

Watch for one way the ECK (Holy Spirit) is helping you in your life. This help may come in countless ways—an insight, guidance, or feeling of upliftment. And it may appear in your daily life, spiritual exercises, and dreams.

The divine power does care about the smallest detail of our being. (pp. 8–9)

1

The Easy Way

$\asterism$

The road to God is the adventure of a lifetime—many lifetimes, in fact. Yet most of us have not found it to be so. Perhaps the reason is that few people have any real idea of what a spiritual life is, so they are hardly able to make the most of it.

First, the teachings of ECK have come to you by design and not by chance. A divine plan has been at work on your behalf for years, to prepare you for the spiritual works of ECK today. Second, most people now in ECK were not wildly unhappy with their lives before. They just felt there was something more. Third, others have come into ECKANKAR because they saw in it certain truths they had already discovered on their own and now wanted to learn more about them.

The Easy Way Discourses are a preview of what lies ahead for you. Yes, there is an easier way to find God, an easier one than you have known before. There is indeed a better, more adventurous way to be a spiritual person, a way that explains the whys of the up-and-down times of daily living.

And what are the stepping-stones in ECK? How can you hope to achieve a better, more productive life with a study of ECK?

The steps are knowledge, wisdom, love, and freedom. The way to reach these states is through the Spiritual Exercises of ECK. Soon you can better handle your roles at home and work, through a fuller grasp of yourself as the author of your own worlds. So every month, these discourses offer you a special exercise. Each is easy as well as enlightening.

In time, your heart and Spiritual Eye will begin to open, like flowers in the warm sunshine of spring. Then you will find delight in the Light and Sound of God too.

Turning Points

Life is a series of turning points. We are sometimes like a railroad car that is part of a train going in a direction we do not wish to go. This train can be our religion.

Eventually, this train we belong to comes to a railroad yard, and we find ourselves at a turning point in life. In the roundhouse, an engineer puts us in a stall on a massive turntable, which rotates until we are headed in a new direction. Then he rolls us off. Shortly, we are rolling out of the railroad yard, but this time we're part of another train, taking a whole new direction in life.

Look back sometime and retrace some early turning points in your own life.

At the time they occurred, they likely tangled you up so in the rush of the moment that you probably had no time to think about their spiritual impact. And that's true of most who come to ECK. Yet these points in time are important, for each occurs at a crucial moment and is an eloquent tribute to the hand of God in our life. The divine

8

power does care about the smallest detail of our being.

So look back sometime. At given points in your life, an invisible force took control of events and by some miracle sent you more in the direction of ECK.

Moving toward ECK

There were many such episodes in my own life. Often too minor to stand out at the time, they nevertheless proved to be major turning points. For example, after I quit my study for the ministry and left college, I returned home to the farm for the summer. My oldest brother was also home. He'd just completed four years of service with the air force and was trying to decide his future.

The summer farmwork was hard, and working with my father was often anything but pleasant, but I loved being close to nature again after so many months in the city.

Yet there was a cloud. As a student for the ministry, I was exempt from military service, but my deferment had now run out. The army could call at any time. One day that summer, the mail carrier dropped the mail off at our farm as usual, and in the mail was a notice from the government that upgraded my draft status from inactive to active. The news upset me badly. The United States was getting more involved in Vietnam, and it wanted thousands of recruits to fill the ranks there.

My thoughts ran back to the church school where I had spent the last eight years. Had I made a mistake? At least in the ministry, I would not have to risk a jungle full of enemy soldiers, each armed and wishing me harm. Besides, this was the first summer that our family had all been together in four years. I decided to share my misgivings about service with my older brother.

"I did my time," he said, "and so can you."

The summer passed all too quickly. While helping my family with chores, making hay, and threshing, the options about my future ran through my head constantly. Life at school had been serene and predictable. The farm was a haven of peace too. It offered an ideal shelter from life, my own model of Thoreau at Walden Pond. So I put off a decision about military service, only because I simply did not know what course to take.

Then one day, there was another letter in the mailbox. It was from the air force recruiter in town, and he was full of ideas. But it was urgent to see him immediately.

God's Subtle Influence

During this entire summer, God was at once near and far from my thoughts. Any influence God might have upon events did not appear to extend to a situation as minor as a meeting with a recruiter. This was the real world. God, church, and faith were for some other place— like the safe and protected harbor of a church campus. But I needed help now. At most, God was only a reality in some other world, and very out of place in the violent kingdom of the military.

The recruiter turned out to be a warm, pleasant man. He gave my options in a few carefully chosen words: "Four years in the air force and you'll have skills when you're home again. Otherwise, it's the army and Vietnam."

A week or so later, I was on a bus headed for Milwaukee. Along the way, our driver stopped in other towns to pick up young men who also had orders to undergo tests for physical and mental fitness for service. Loud soldiers at a military center in Milwaukee herded us into classrooms like flocks of sheep. There was nothing soft or genteel about their manner. And after the written tests, other guides took us to an area where doctors gave us the medical exams.

It was here that my life reached one of those minor turning points that most of us seldom recognize, even years later.

A young doctor gave me a battery of tests, poking and prodding my body like a cattle buyer who wants to purchase a sound animal. Everything was fine until he took my pulse and blood pressure. My heart raced wildly. It was beating fast, like the heart of a rabbit my brothers and I had caught one summer while threshing oats.

So I had failed the medical exam.

The doctor who had examined me left the room and returned with two other doctors. They studied me with care. I sat quietly before them on the medical table, with a pressure cuff loosely on my arm, worried about my future. It suddenly became clear that the farm would eventually choke the life from me, and that my only hope for a future was to pass this physical exam. Asking me to lie down on a cot to rest, the doctors then left the room.

When the first doctor returned a half hour later, I was nearly asleep. He quickly fixed the cuff on my arm again, squeezed the hand pump, then read the gauge. All was normal.

"Nothing the matter with you," he said cheerily. "Have a nice four years."

Those extra thirty minutes on the doctor's cot, in an otherwise very ordinary day, were indeed a major turning point in my life. But it was years before I realized the full impact of that day. The military was to give me the freedom and means to explore the spiritual life at my leisure. None of that would have happened on the farm.

And would I have found ECK?

In this next year of spiritual study, we will touch upon some of the more dramatic and interesting facets of ECK like Soul Travel, dreams, karma, reincarnation, and the ancient science of prophecy. You will also gain a golden insight into spiritual healing, the ECK initiations, and the God Worlds of ECK. All these areas are necessary for a traveler on the road home to God. But you will find the most spiritual benefit in the secrets of the Sound and Light. We will cover those too.

Learning the Life of ECK

While it is certainly true that you are about to embark upon a unique adventure into the spiritual worlds of being, ECKANKAR is, above all, a path to help you fit into life. The fast pace today hardly lends itself to a solitary existence. Anyway, there is little or no reason to be a hermit, because this world is to teach us how to love and serve God, as well as our fellow creatures.

So instead, seek love, wisdom, freedom, and understanding. And through your daily efforts with the Spiritual Exercises of ECK, you will become a pure and holy channel for God, a Co-worker of the highest order.

Yes, Soul Travel and dreams are a useful part of the ECK teachings. But set your sights higher. As a member of ECKANKAR, you belong to a spiritual community that covers the entire planet, but its reach goes far beyond. And usually, you want to live in the present moment—here and now. Our past is seldom more than rooms and rooms full of arid images, thoughts, or feelings. Yet sometimes we do look back. After all, the seed of our present life hides in the past, where we may look for understanding in the face of trouble.

Take the following case:

Tracy, in a relationship with a young man, was happy enough with her situation. In fact, she nearly took her happiness for granted. All went well until recently, when he started to press her into marriage so the couple could begin a family. But she was not that sold upon their relationship right then. Finally, she did give in.

A few days later, her partner had second thoughts about the marriage, having children, or even about their staying together.

In just a moment, her world exploded.

Shocked by the sudden change of events, Tracy couldn't settle down long enough to even do a spiritual exercise. But a friend of hers, an ESA, held two spiritual aide sessions with her. An ESA is an ECK Spiritual Aide: a High Initiate of ECK and member of the ECK clergy appointed by the Mahanta, the Living ECK Master who listens to a person in need of help. The ESA mostly listens. But in the meantime, the Holy Spirit, or ECK, begins to act upon the problem and brings about a solution or an understanding of it.

In the second session, by phone, the ESA told Tracy to chant *Kalam*. A spiritual word that means the Sound Current, it is another term for the Light and Sound of God, or the ECK. He said it would help relax her.

She hung up the phone. Desperate for any sort of help, she began to sing the word quietly to herself. Almost immediately, a calm came over her. The next day, she could sit down long enough to try a more formal spiritual exercise, again by singing Kalam (KAH-LAHM). She began to picture herself on the Physical Plane with the Mahanta. The same method took her up to the Astral Plane, the seat of human emotions.

13

Suddenly, the Mahanta stood before her. He started to lift her past the Causal Plane, just beyond the Astral, but she asked if she could examine her past-life records stored there.

Was there a past-life reason for all the pain Tracy was feeling about the chance that she and her partner might go their separate ways?

The scene changed. A stack of index file cards suddenly appeared before her. Then she saw a room decorated in a motif of tiny Victorian flowers: the wallpaper, the bedspread, a nightstand, the easy chair, and even the pillows. A fresh breeze blew in the window.

Tracy, in that lifetime, was a child of ten. And as she looked out through the window, she saw horses and lush rolling pastures, where she often loved to ride. The time frame was the South, a few years before the American Civil War. The scene shifted once more. It was now later in that same lifetime, and Tracy was a young woman. She had a deep love for a soldier (also her partner now) who left her to fight for the South. But later, he switched his allegiance to the North and never came back for her. The pain and heartbreak of that lost love was staggering, and she spent the rest of that lifetime longing for his love.

Now she knew the reason for her original fear of their marriage.

As she sat in her chair for a few minutes more, she recalled a letter she had written to the Mahanta, the Living ECK Master about her heartbreak. The shock of her partner changing his mind about marriage had allowed her desire for truth to emerge.

"Show it all to me," she had said.

And very quickly the Mahanta did, letting her see the reason for her resistance to this marriage so she could deal with it.

This Month's Exercise

The spiritual exercise for this month is "The Easy Way." It is similar to one that Paul Twitchell, the founder of ECKANKAR, gave years ago to the early students of ECK. It goes like this:

Make yourself comfortable in a chair, on a couch, or even in bed. Shut your eyes, look in the Third Eye: a point roughly above and behind your eyebrows. Then sing *Kalam* or *HU*, an ancient name for God, in one long breath. Repeat it slowly. Do this for fifteen to twenty minutes, then quit, and try it again the next day if nothing happens. It sometimes takes a little longer to meet the Mahanta in full awareness. But you will before long.

Workbook Activities

1.   *A divine plan has been at work on your behalf for years, to prepare you for the spiritual works of ECK today. . . . Others have come into ECKANKAR because they saw in it certain truths they had already discovered on their own and now wanted to learn more about them.* (p. 7)

You've already discovered certain truths that have led you here. As you read lesson 1 throughout the month, more truths may catch your attention. You can highlight or underline them for future reference.

A technique to meet the Mahanta, the Inner Master, in full awareness awaits you at the top of this page.

2.   *There is indeed a better, more adventurous way to be a spiritual person, a way that explains the whys of the up-and-down times of daily living.* (p. 7)

What's one key you've found in this lesson to help you on your spiritual quest? It may be a phrase or image that sticks with you. Or something that raises questions and makes you curious. You can circle it or draw a star by it. Or you can jot it down here.

Turning Points (pp. 8–9)

3.   *Life is a series of turning points. We are some-*
        times like a railroad car that is part of a train going
        in a direction we do not wish to go. This train can
        be our religion.

        Eventually, this train we belong to comes to a
        railroad yard, and we find ourselves at a turning
        point in life. In the roundhouse, an engineer puts us
        in a stall on a massive turntable, which rotates until
        we are headed in a new direction. (p. 8)

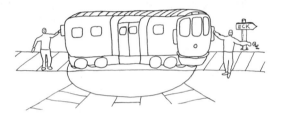

You'll find an example of a turning point on pages
8–12.

Then take a moment to look back on your own
life. Ask the Mahanta, the inner teacher, to show
you one of your turning points: a time when an
invisible force took control of events and sent you
more in the direction of ECK. You can write about
it here.

4. The following quote gives a preview of this year's study. What topics are of special interest to you? Feel free to underline or highlight them here.

> *In this next year of spiritual study, we will touch upon some of the more dramatic and interesting facets of ECK like Soul Travel, dreams, karma, reincarnation, and the ancient science of prophecy. You will also gain a golden insight into spiritual healing, the ECK initiations, and the God Worlds of ECK. All these areas are necessary for a traveler on the road home to God. But you will find the most spiritual benefit in the secrets of the Sound and Light. We will cover those too.* (p. 12)

Would you like the Mahanta, the Inner Master, to show you more about a topic during the coming year? You can write a brief note of invitation to him here. It can be fun and illuminating to reread this note at the end of the year.

Learning the Life of ECK (pp. 12–14)

5.   *The seed of our present life hides in the past,
          where we may look for understanding in the face of
          trouble.* (p. 12)

In the story on pages 13–14, Tracy faces a difficult
challenge in her personal life that has seeds in a
past life. Reflect for a moment on a challenge in
your life. Do you feel it might relate to a past life?
If you wish, ask the Mahanta, the Living ECK
Master for more understanding of this situation.

6.   *The Holy Spirit, or ECK, begins to act upon the
          problem and brings about a solution or an under-
          standing of it.* (p. 13)

Tracy does a spiritual exercise to examine her
past-life records and finds a reason for her current
challenge. If this is of interest to you, read the
exercise on pages 13–14 and go through the steps
yourself.

You can jot down your experiences here, if you
wish.

7.   *Seek love, wisdom, freedom, and understanding. And through your daily efforts with the Spiritual Exercises of ECK, you will become a pure and holy channel for God, a Co-worker of the highest order.* (p. 12)

Take a moment to imagine being a pure and holy channel for God, a Co-worker of the highest order. How does it feel? How do you think, talk, and act?

This Month's Exercise

A technique to meet the Mahanta
in full awareness, p. 15

8. 🎧 **Audio Excerpt 2**

You can listen to a child's experience with the
Sound and Light of ECK in this excerpt from
the talk "True Wisdom."

As you do the spiritual exercise on page 15
every day, awareness of the Mahanta, the
Inner Master, may come during contemplation, in your daily life, or in your dreams.

Here are some ways to be aware of the
Mahanta that are shared in a book for Second
Initiates and above, yet this brief passage may
help you now as well. You can highlight or
underline ones you have experienced. Be open
to discovering your own unique ways.

> *When you put your attention on the Inner
> Master or you sing one of the sacred sounds
> of God, it opens you to the love of Divine
> Spirit. You might get goose bumps or a feeling
> of warmth that settles on you like a coat. Your
> face may get flushed. This is the presence of
> the Master, the protection and love that you
> have opened yourself to.*
>
> *Often, before you see the Blue Light or
> hear one of the sounds, you may have a
> knowingness and assurance of the Master's
> presence. I would say a higher way of being in*

the life of ECK is seeing Spirit at work with you in your daily life.

—*Be the HU: How to Become a Co-worker with God,* pp. 43–44

What's one experience of upliftment or divine love that you had during this month?

Extra Writing Page
for this month's exercises and experiences

The difference was that the Sound was now humming right through her, in her weightless and drifting state. The Sound carried her along. She felt wonderful. (p. 31)

2

In Soul You Are Free

✳

*I*n 1968, Brad Steiger's *In My Soul I Am Free* hit the bookstores and caused a sensation among those with an interest in psychic matters. For me, it was a godsend. I had known about Paul Twitchell and ECKANKAR for a year, but this book, in my mind anyway, gave a legitimacy to Paul Twitchell and the teachings of ECK.

In My Soul I Am Free. The sound of that title was like music, exciting a spirit of love and adventure unlike anything I had ever felt before, surpassing even my first encounter with ECKANKAR.

For the first time, I felt like a part of something bigger and more grand. The world was an oyster in my hands. More than ever, I recognized the jewel of wisdom that hid in the writings of ECK, because they held the key to the secret worlds of God. Anyone who could enter them, I believed, would find joy and happiness in all stations of life. Saint Paul's words to the Philippians came to mind: "For I have learned, in whatsoever state I am, therewith to be content."

To be honest, I felt no great desire to learn Soul Travel for its true purpose: to reach God-Realization. I did not understand the term. All I cared about was learning how to move to distant places on earth, flying through time and space like a flash of lightning, and mingling in crowds there in my invisible body. That sort of freedom was very appealing to me at the time.

What about all those stories of people who learned to Soul Travel? Were they true?

It can be annoying to hear about people who succeed wildly in a field of special ability, like Soul Travel, when our own efforts seem such failures. We wonder, *How long do I keep the faith? What is a reasonable time to wait for an experience out of the body, and when it comes, will I be ready?*

The Unique Nature of Soul

The ECK teachings point to the unique nature of Soul. It means that you, I, and every other person in the world are one of a kind. The mold from which we are cast is one that changes with each experience we ever have—from our very first life on earth to the present. So people have many traits, those of love, suspicion, trust, fear, jealousy, spirit, and more.

As Rebazar Tarzs, the ECK Master, once said: Only the bold and adventuresome find God.

To Learn Soul Travel

How long, then, does it take to learn Soul Travel? It depends upon you. If you love and trust in God, then you will find Soul Travel to be an easy skill to master. Fear and suspicion will hold you back spiritually.

We all dream of an experience like that of Marie (not

her real name), because it has all the elements of Soul Travel in the right order.

One Saturday night, Marie prepared for bed. Before going to sleep, she decided to chant *HU*, an ancient love song to God. Feeling very open to the love of SUGMAD (God) and the Mahanta, she suddenly heard a loud vibrating Sound, while the room filled with white and colored rings of Light that swirled around her. Then a gentle force lifted her from her body. There was a pulling sensation from her head down to her legs, but then she felt a strong wave of love to counter some of the anxiety that had risen.

She tried to Soul Travel farther from her physical body and chanted *HU*, but at that point, the experience ended.

Marie makes no claims to being a saint. When she first became a member of ECKANKAR, she was in the habit of closing her eyes to problems and shortcomings, but now she is learning to take charge of her life. Yet even those who choose the high road to God often find their spiritual progress will wax and wane.

What irks some people, myself included, is getting a newsletter from some group that professes to teach its students a certain skill—like a home business. The newsletter is full of testimonials. But the average person does not find success so readily as the people in the testimonials claim to have, and so the reader feels a sense of betrayal.

The same problem might occur in ECKANKAR. There is always the tension between the state of consciousness a person is at here and now compared to a higher one he could attain with a little more effort and self-discipline.

Many people are spiritually lazy. In fact, the bulk of humanity fits into that class, for it is much safer to stay quiet and not risk rocking the boat among family and friends. The main fear people have is of being different, because anyone who decides to leave the herd and take an independent course in life will surely be the target of verbal arrows. Such an attack can be cruel, especially when the change is about wanting to join a new religion.

A record of my own success with Soul Travel is in several books, among them *The Wind of Change, Soul Travelers of the Far Country, Child in the Wilderness,* and *Autobiography of a Modern Prophet.* Yet perhaps I, too, omit speaking of my setbacks on the path of ECK.

Certainly, there were many.

My intention is never to downplay a failure but simply to set your sights high, upon the vision of what you also can hope to achieve through the ECK teachings. Yes, I did Soul Travel on many occasions and saw sights and wonders beyond words. But how do I paint a picture of the love, self-discipline, and trust that made it possible?

To learn a skill, you must work at it. If you want to become better than average at it, you must make a greater effort. What about a world-class champion? This person, whatever the field, has let his interest become a passion: in fact, an obsession. Later, the crowds may envy the star. They mimic a star's hairstyle and manner of speaking or walking, but no one would ever mistake them for the star. The imitator lacks the awards, the bearing, and above all, the self-discipline that brought riches and fame to the celebrity.

A trait of the crowd is imitation, but you want to get above that.

The question is, How?

Set Your Sights on God

First, set your sights on a goal no less than God Consciousness itself. Yes, the ECK teachings do recognize the need for people to have food, shelter, and clothing—and

28

these can be yours in abundance. For God loves the rich and the poor alike. Yet the spiritual goal of living is far beyond the mere gathering of goods and coins, as a miser would, and hoarding them in a safe place. Ahead of anything else, put your sights on God. Do that, and you will find that the events of your life will begin to appear in the right order.

What did I want from ECKANKAR when I first learned about it in 1967?

Soul Travel was the single most important facet to strike me about the early ECK teachings, so I put all my time and energy into getting out of the body. Often, in contemplation, I would hear and feel a sound similar to the one Marie described above. The Sound changed from time to time. It was usually like lying on a vibrating bed in a hotel, except that only my body, and not the bed, would vibrate to a steady humming noise.

It used to cause me some anxiety and often brought a quick end to the experience.

So I spent a lot of time first asking Paul Twitchell inwardly for the experience, then chiding myself when it came and my fears scared it off. But no matter how often I failed, I always tried again. Fear, so deeply ingrained in me, took over until I had sincere doubts at my ability to ever Soul Travel. Yet I was like a bulldog. That may sound like a feeble attempt to be dramatic, but I refused to ever give up. So many people do. If they see no immediate result after a few days at a Spiritual Exercise of ECK, they want to quit.

Spirit of Adventure

But others sense the love and truth in ECK and display even more self-discipline. Jenny (not her real name) is an example of one who has this spirit of adventure, and it is

29

people like that who Soul Travel and catch other secrets of the spiritual arts.

Jenny admits having a fearful nature. And it is just that attitude, she knows, which has so often kept her from having the Soul Travel experiences she desires. But one night she was doing the spiritual exercise mentioned in that month's discourse. It was late, and she was about to go to sleep for the night. During her contemplation, she mentioned to Wah Z (the spiritual name of the Mahanta, the Living ECK Master) her wish to have an experience of some kind. She wanted to know more about the nature of Soul.

After making her appeal, she turned out the light, prepared for sleep, and completely forgot about the request. Then she filled her thoughts with love.

Of course, Jenny did not understand the value of love for having a Soul Travel experience. So her thoughts lingered upon the image of a new acquaintance, a man she had fallen in love with. In her imagination, she told him of her love. As she rolled over in bed and was ready to go to sleep, a most peculiar action began to occur. For starters, she did not fall asleep. Or even doze off. Fully awake and conscious of her body motionless on the bed, she suddenly felt herself drift away from her resting body.

My consciousness is about to go to a higher level, she thought. *I asked for it, and here it comes. I must go ahead.*

Then her consciousness (Soul)—rather, she—went farther from the physical body, idly drifting away. Everything was dark. Jenny chose not to open her eyes because of fear that it would spoil the experience and put her back inside her physical body again.

She wondered, *Am I floating above or below my body?*

Her curiosity grew. She realized that her distance or position from the physical body was of no real importance, so she turned her attention to other parts of the Soul Travel experience. She then became aware of the Sound of God, which for her was usually a deep, constant hum. It was especially loud that night. The difference was that the Sound was now humming right through her, in her weightless and drifting state. The Sound carried her along. She felt wonderful.

Jenny was in the Soul body, a unit of divine Light, and the Sound of God vibrated Its love throughout her. It was all she needed.

Happy, she cried out, "Mahanta, this is fantastic!"

Her thoughts now returned to the physical body at rest on the bed. Outside her body, Jenny sent a command to move one of her fingers to see how much control she could exercise over her physical shell. Her finger did move as she had expected. Then she felt a pull upon her, as Soul, to return to the human form, and her Soul Travel experience was over.

Jenny felt somewhat sad to see it end.

Back in the heaviness of her earthly body, Jenny reflected upon other, very short Soul Travel experiences in the past. Each time she became aware of her absence from the body, she would instantly return to it.

Something Wah Z once said now came to mind: "The human body is like a portable hole that the unenlightened Soul carries around to hide in, not daring to go anywhere without it." That night, Jenny had dared to leave it for a few minutes. Most of all, she had felt trust. It was all so quiet and peaceful that she could control the experience, which left her with a sense of harmony and joy.

Upon her return to the physical body, she found a smile upon her lips. *If this is like dying,* she thought, *how could I ever be afraid of death?*

Indeed, one purpose of Soul Travel is to give proof of life beyond death of the physical body.

Meet Yourself as Soul

My goal in this discourse is simply to introduce you to yourself as Soul, made in the image and likeness of God.

An error that so many people make is that the physical body is the mirror of the Most High, yet that, of course, only shows their ignorance about the nature of Soul. No one can say with any certainty what God is. However, we do know that God makes Itself known to us through Its Light and Sound, which the Christian faith speaks of as the Holy Ghost and other names. Yet the Holy Spirit is not a person in the sense of a human being. It is the action of divine Sound and Light. As such, It is the Voice of God. And Soul is also of Light and Sound.

The awakened Soul is in tune with God, yet such an individual is nearly as rare as a white eagle. You can reach those heights too.

Do you wish to unfold spiritually, find love, and perhaps even Soul Travel? The first step is to fill your heart, mind, and body with gratitude, for that is a true expression of love.

How do you find love?

In *Stranger by the River*, ECK Master Rebazar Tarzs tells the seeker: "Therefore, if you desire love, try to realize that the only way to get love is by giving love."

This Month's Exercise

Here's an easy technique you may try for Soul Travel. First, choose a quiet time and place, where no one is likely to disturb you for ten or twenty minutes. Second, think of someone you love very much, until your heart opens in gratitude. Third, take a comfortable seat on a couch, bed, chair, or even the floor. Last, shut your eyes, look gently at a point between your eyebrows, and sing *HU* (like the word *hue*) in one long, soft syllable.

After some trial periods that may take a month or longer, you will have some experience to show you the true nature of Soul. Look for a Light in the darkness. Listen for a Sound, musical or otherwise.

If you see a Light or hear an inner Sound, you will be in the Divine Presence.

Then be still and listen.

Workbook Activities

1.   In My Soul I Am Free. *The sound of that title was like music, exciting a spirit of love and adventure unlike anything I had ever felt before, surpassing even my first encounter with ECKANKAR.*
(p. 25)

Remember the last time you had a heart-to-heart chat with a close friend? As you sit down to read this month's lesson, imagine you're having a chat like that with the Mahanta, the Inner Master. And he's speaking these words directly to you. What catches your attention? You can highlight or underline those parts of the discourse, or note them here.

You'll find an easy technique for Soul Travel in this month's exercise on pages 32–33.

2. The following quote gives some exciting benefits of Soul Travel. You can highlight or underline the things that are of special interest to you.

> *To be honest, I felt no great desire to learn Soul Travel for its true purpose: to reach God-Realization. I did not understand the term. All I cared about was learning how to move to distant places on earth, flying through time and space like a flash of lightning, and mingling in crowds there in my invisible body. That sort of freedom was very appealing to me at the time.* (p. 26)

What other benefits of Soul Travel would you like to experience?

To Learn Soul Travel (pp. 26–27)

3.　　　*Feeling very open to the love of SUGMAD (God)
and the Mahanta, she suddenly heard a loud vibrating Sound, while the room filled with white and
colored rings of Light that swirled around her. Then
a gentle force lifted her from her body.* (pp. 26–27)

Stretch your imagination! Read Marie's story on
page 27, and imagine that her experience is happening to you.

Then draw a simple cartoon of yourself above
your physical body on the bed. Imagine the freedom you would feel. What do you now know
about yourself as Soul? As a divine being? You
can write your insight in the balloon.

4.   *To learn a skill, you must work at it. If you want
          to become better than average at it, you must make
          a greater effort.* (p. 28)

Here are some tips for Soul Travel. Look over
the three experiences given on pages 26–31. Ask
the Mahanta, the inner teacher, to point out something that will be of special help to you. You can
write it here.

Meet Yourself as Soul (p. 32)

5.   *My goal in this discourse is simply to introduce you to yourself as Soul, made in the image and likeness of God.* (p. 31)

Enjoy this special exercise. Silently ask the Mahanta, the Inner Master, to help you become more aware of yourself, made in the image and likeness of God.

Then imagine that the Mahanta sends a personal greeting to you as Soul. Write whatever you perceive here.

Dear _____ ,
　　　　　(your name)

6.   The spiritual exercise for this month is on pages
     32–33. It begins in a very enjoyable way:

     *Think of someone you love very much, until
     your heart opens in gratitude.* (pp. 32–33)

     Think of one person or thing you love very much.
     To help open your heart, jot down some reasons
     you're grateful for having that person or thing in
     your life.

This Month's Exercise

An easy technique to try for Soul Travel, pp. 32–33

7.   *Look for a Light in the darkness. Listen for a Sound, musical or otherwise.*
        If you see a Light or hear an inner Sound, you will be in the Divine Presence.
        Then be still and listen. (p. 33)

Try the easy exercise on pages 32–33 for ten or twenty minutes every day. What is the Divine Presence saying to you?

Audio Excerpt 3

For another example of a Soul Travel experience, you can listen to this excerpt from the talk "Just for Love."

Spotlight on ECK (Holy Spirit):
Noticing and Remembering the Spiritual Gifts

8.   *After some trial periods that may take a month or longer, you will have some experience to show you the true nature of Soul.* (p. 33)

Insights can come to you all during the month through your contemplations, dreams, and daily life experiences. To help bring them to light, at the end of the month you can scan this lesson again or look at the parts you highlighted.

Silently ask the Mahanta, the Inner Master, "What's one insight I've had this month on the true nature of Soul?" Then write a response here.

✎

Extra Writing Page
for this month's exercises and experiences

Extra Writing Page
for this month's exercises and experiences

Dream travel is a talent that saints have used with great success since the dawn of history. So pull open the draperies of your spiritual window—and welcome to the dream worlds of ECK. (p. 53)

3

Dream On,
Sweet Dreamer

✦

*T*here are dreams, and then there are dreams. Frankly, modern society treats the dream world like a fantasy, a figment of the imagination, or some other kind of science fiction. Yet dreams are of utmost importance in ECK.

You are what you dream.

Beyond our world lies a sublime creation filled with beings of every size, shape, and color, but still as real as anyone you could meet, touch, or speak to here. For many, this dream world simply does not exist. That is a shame, for in closing the door on it, they also shut out the wisdom and truth of God.

Don't let this be you.

This morning, as I sat down to write this ECK discourse to you, the draperies of the window in my room were drawn shut against the darkness outside. But later, daylight began to show through the fabric. The faint light piqued my curiosity: What kind of weather did the day hold in store—cold, snow, wind, or sunshine? On impulse,

45

I opened the draperies. A few feet inside the small woodlot behind our home a pheasant, a large and elusive game bird, was at breakfast eating birdseed set out for the feathered members of our family.

Busy, he did not notice me. So it gave me a chance to watch a beautiful creature who is usually off and running at the slightest stir at a window. A few minutes later, finished with breakfast, he slipped from sight into the woods. Only then did I notice the overcast, rainy day.

This quiet morning scene had been there all along, but until I left the keyboard and drew open the draperies, the outside world did not exist for me.

It takes a little effort of the same kind to visit the dream worlds.

The Planes of God

Near the end of this discourse, I will give a brief, simple technique to help you remember your travels into the other planes of God. But first, you must know what to look for.

Anyone who has been in ECKANKAR for any length of time knows that divine creation is split into two parts: the lower and the higher planes. The lower planes are a material realm of time, matter, space, and energy—and the physical plane, of course, belongs here. The higher planes, your spiritual goal whether you know it or not, are that area beyond time and space: the true worlds of God. Let's take a quick tour of these spiritual planes.

The Physical Plane

First is the Physical Plane, a place of unique opportunity, for it is the testing ground of Soul. Sadly, too many people take this plane for granted. It is a privilege for Soul to be here, to take on a human body and to greet with arms

thrown wide the rich experience of living. Yet many regard this life as a curse. They feel that God or fate or
someone else has put them into an evil setting unfit even
for a pig, and the sooner death comes to release them, the
better. But like it or not, earth is a chief part of God's
education system. It is a pressure cooker.

Karma and reincarnation come into play here, but we
will look at them another time. For starters, though, begin
to count your blessings.

The Astral Plane

The Second Plane, the usual destination of people while
asleep at night, is the Astral. An actual plane of existence,
it is also the source of emotion and feeling for people in
everyday life during their waking hours. The Astral Plane
is a higher side of the Physical. In fact, many of the loca-
tions there bear a strong resemblance to places here, yet
they are often of a more highly refined and artistic style.

The reason for this is simple.

Divine law states that each world is an unpolished reflection of a world above it. No wonder, then, that architects
and others who depend upon a stream of fresh ideas in their
professions often come to the Astral world in the dream
state. The original of every design, every piece of art, music,
or literature, and every device may be found on the Astral
Plane. In fact, a favorite place of many new members in ECK
is the astral museum, which houses a wide collection of
pieces to astound even a science-fiction buff. Stephen King,
the prolific and famous novelist, makes regular trips to the
lower Astral regions.

The Causal Plane

Third of the lower worlds is the Causal Plane. Source
of memories, it holds a complete record of your past lives

on the Astral and Physical planes. The foremost cause of human misery and despair is that leaders of the orthodox religions have so little knowledge, if any, about the facts of life—the reason for Soul's exile in the human form.

The Causal Plane is the place of memories, the Hall of Records. A dreamer may ask the Mahanta, the Dream Master, to go there and view the record of his past lives. When the dreamer is spiritually ready for that step, the Mahanta will take him there for that experience, for this plane exists to store and to play back the past as memories.

The Mental Plane

Our fourth stop in this brief excursion through the ECK worlds is the Mental Plane.

Travelers often think of it as the plane of blue colors. The reason is this: Here the Mahanta often appears to a dream traveler as a blue light, one of the road marks of the Mental Plane. But this region actually enjoys a full spectrum of light as do the Physical, Astral, and Causal planes. The difference here is that the light is far more clear, bright, and beautiful than in any of the cosmic regions below. And why is that? This purity of light and substance occurs because the Mental Plane is close to the Soul Plane, the first of the true spiritual regions, which lies just beyond.

The Mental Plane is home to billions of Souls. It is their base of operations. Odd as it may appear, there are few travelers who come here from earth with any regularity, since most people have trouble getting beyond their emotions. They like the Astral Plane better.

The inhabitants of the Mental Plane, and its visitors, are usually of high mental development. Do not confuse mental development with ethics, for even the Mental Plane is still another classroom in the divine scheme, giving Souls the chance to gain the traits of love, wisdom, and spiritual power. Some people who live there do misuse their abilities. They are merely Souls with superior mental powers who still need to find the qualities of love and compassion before they can rise to being Co-workers with God.

What sort of person comes to the Mental Plane?

People who have come to the Mental Plane via dream travel include thinkers like Einstein, musicians like Mozart, artists like Michelangelo. Other dream travelers are those who develop the inventions of others or their own into systems, like Edison or Ford. This group also includes some leaders of countries and religions, but very many more in education. That should be of no surprise.

The Etheric Plane

The Etheric Plane lies just beyond the Mental worlds. Since the Etheric Plane is actually a part of the high Mental Plane, we count it there. Each plane has a sacred word that acts like a sort of a key to unlock the mysteries found there, and on the Etheric Plane it is *baju* (BAH-joo). Sing this word sometime during a spiritual exercise and see what happens.

This plane is the seat of intuition. Source of the unconscious mind, it is the place where all dreams begin, for it is a most delicate area of high transparency. Its function is to act as a buffer between the pure spiritual worlds above and the impure material worlds below. The etheric mind is a creation of this world. It serves to protect the human mind from any shocks, like the reason behind a person's need to reincarnate in the present life. For this reason, another name for the etheric mind is the censor. It will step in to prevent one from seeing a past life if the shock of that lifetime might upset the routine of an individual.

The censor is both a bane and a blessing. While it might shield a person from his past behavior, a knowledge of past deeds will usually help an individual move ahead spiritually. In that case, the Mahanta steps in. He will override the censor and let the individual see a past life in the dream state or by some other means, so the ECK initiate can get on with his life.

The Soul Plane

The Fifth Plane is the Soul Plane. This area provides a major turning point.

The Soul Plane is the first of the true spiritual worlds, and this level should be your first target in ECK. It is here that the Mahanta opens the petals of your heart more than you ever imagined possible, for this is the plane of the ECKshar. Here you reach the state of Self-Realization. This state brings a state of consciousness higher than any you have ever known, giving in the clearest possible sense a true picture of what your purpose is in life.

This realization, which comes on the Soul Plane, is unknown to the followers of most other religions, who go only as far as the Mental Plane in their pursuit of God. On the Fifth Plane, and in the planes above that, the pure Sound and Light of God can better uplift and strengthen your heart. All who love God shall one day come here. I won't say more now, except that the word you may sing for the Soul Plane is *SUGMAD* (SOOG-mahd).

It is the name of the Formless One, the God of All.

Access to the Inner Worlds

You will find a unique character to your dreams on each of these planes. Nightmares occur on the Astral Plane, but so do many happy and enjoyable dreams. It all depends upon the individual, for some people place themselves in the lower Astral regions by reason of drunkenness, anger, gluttony, greed, or other habits brought on by poor self-discipline.

A child's nightmares, common before age five, occur mostly because the mind is still in an undeveloped state. So when the etheric censor sees a past-life experience coming up for review that is sure to upset the child, the censor is helpless. The child still has too few mental habits that the censor can redeploy to use as barriers to block out frightening dreams. Once a child begins school, and the forces of education begin to make an impression upon him, the nightmares often occur less often. The child is developing a material mind.

So it is education that closes out his or her ready access to the inner planes, where seeing, knowing, and being are the hallmarks of Soul.

For most, the window of Soul remains barred for a lifetime. Dreams get pushed into the background. As a child gets older, he or she usually finds that no one wants to hear about them, neither parents nor friends. So the child forgets.

At my elementary school, there was a girl who used to have a rich dream life. Often when she came to school, she would say, "Last night I dreamed . . . " Then she would tell her dream. The trouble was none of us wanted to listen, because recess was too short the way it was. So we ran off to play. The little dreamer spoke less of her dreams as she got older and entered into the higher grades. The other children soon came to ignore the girl and her dreams, simply because that is what they had learned from their parents. At home, few of the families ever talked about dreams, because they felt the inner life had no bearing upon anything.

A Doorway to Truth

In ECK, dreams are one of the highlights of an ECKist's life, because the Mahanta uses them to give an insight into the subtleties of life. Dreams can show the future, the cause of illness, the reason for problems in a relationship, and more. Dreams are the last frontier.

While dreams are a Mr. Fixit for someone who has learned how to interpret them, they have yet another side. They are a handy way to explore new realms of consciousness. First the individual must stand back and make a fresh appraisal of who and what he is—and also what he wants from life. The purpose of life is to learn and earn the qualities of Spirit. Dreams are a doorway to truth. Yet it takes a seeker time and patience before he is ready to accept the fruit of the dream world offered to him.

Soul can exist in many worlds at once. A dream is simply a memory of a person's travels in the other planes, and they provide many experiences and insights to teach him how to run things better here. An ECKist with the right spiritual training can learn to manage his problems and will not use dreams as an escape.

This Month's Exercise

This discourse is only an introduction to dreams. There is a more in-depth study available through the ECK dream discourses, but you can get a head start on the study of dreams now.

The ECK study of dreams is simple. The only requirement is that you do a Spiritual Exercise of ECK daily and jot down a few notes about any dream you remember, plus your best guess as to its meaning. That's all there is to it. To get you off in the right direction, here is an exercise for you to try tonight:

Before bedtime, sit in a comfortable chair or lie down in bed. Very quietly, or even silently, begin to sing the universal name for God, *SUGMAD*. Sing it for five minutes, keeping your eyes shut and your attention fixed gently upon the Spiritual Eye, the place between your eyebrows. Open your heart to love and goodwill.

After five minutes of doing this exercise, quit singing and just sit still for another ten or fifteen minutes. Keep your eyes gently shut, however. Then look for the Blue Light of the Mahanta, because it is of the Holy Spirit. And don't give in to worry, because the Dream Master is always on hand in the Soul body to keep watch over you.

After twenty minutes, you may open your eyes. Then go to sleep as usual.

Dream travel is a talent that saints have used with great success since the dawn of history. So pull open the draperies of your spiritual window—and welcome to the dream worlds of ECK.

Workbook Activities

1.　　*Beyond our world lies a sublime creation filled with beings of every size, shape, and color, but still as real as anyone you could meet, touch, or speak to here.* (p. 45)

Imagine you're meeting with the Mahanta, the Inner Master. He's revealing special dream information—just for you—as you read this lesson and underline key points. See if you can summarize these insights in a few words or sentences.

Want to remember your dream travels in the God worlds? The spiritual exercise for this month, on pages 52–53, will help you.

The Planes of God (p. 46)

2.   *Near the end of this discourse, I will give a brief,*
         simple technique to help you remember your travels
         into the other planes of God. But first, you must
         know what to look for.
         . . . Let's take a quick tour of these spiritual planes.
         (p. 46)

🎧 Audio Excerpt 4

You can also listen to this excerpt from "The
Dream Master, Part 1."

Are you ready for a spiritual geography lesson?
Take a tour of the planes of God on pages 46–50.

When you find something of special interest about
a plane, you can jot it down below. This may help
you recognize where your dream journeys have led
you as you travel through these worlds of God
every night.

✎

The Physical Plane (pp. 46–47)

The Physical Plane (continued)

The Astral Plane (p. 47)

The Causal Plane (pp. 47–48)

✎

The Mental Plane (pp. 48–49)

The Etheric Plane (pp. 49–50)

☆ Tip: A sacred word is given for you to sing to
unlock the mysteries of the Etheric Plane. You'll
find it on page 49.

The Soul Plane (p. 50)

3. The word to use for this month's spiritual exercise is *SUGMAD* (SOOG-mahd). It's the sacred word—the key—to unlock the mysteries of the Soul Plane.

> *The Soul Plane is the first of the true spiritual worlds, and this level should be your first target in ECK. It is here that the Mahanta opens the petals of your heart more than you ever imagined possible.* (p. 50)

Imagine that the Mahanta, the inner teacher, is telling you about the Soul Plane as you review that section on page 50. What lights up for you?

Access to the Inner Worlds (pp. 50–51)

4.   *You will find a unique character to your dreams on each of these planes.* (p. 50)

Let's explore. Look over the dreams you had this month and pick one. Which plane do you think your dream took place on?

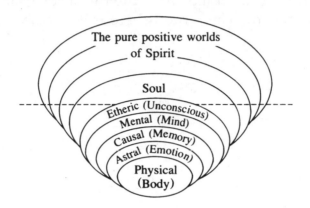

What message did you get from your dream?

A Doorway to Truth (p. 52)

5.   *First the individual must stand back and make a fresh appraisal of who and what he is—and also what he wants from life.* (p. 52)

Try this experiment. Look at yourself in a mirror. Ask yourself, Who and what are you? What do you want from life? And then wait for your answer. You can write it here if you wish.

6.   *Open your heart to love and goodwill.* (p. 53)

What are some ways you've found to open your heart to love? To goodwill? You can write them here. You can also use your imagination and creativity to jot down some new ways to open your heart.

Try one of these ways to open your heart as you do your daily spiritual exercise.

This Month's Exercise

A technique for dream travel, pp. 52–53

7.   *The ECK study of dreams is simple. The only requirement is that you do a Spiritual Exercise of ECK daily and jot down a few notes about any dream you remember, plus your best guess as to its meaning.* (p. 52)

You can jot down or sketch any images and feelings from your dreams here or in your journal. Also, add the meaning and insights you got from your dream here, in your journal, or on page 64.

Tips:

- Keep paper and pen handy by your bed.

- Jot down any perceptions as soon as you awake.

- Even if you don't remember a dream, write down any feelings and insights. You may surprise yourself!

Spotlight on ECK (Holy Spirit):
Noticing and Remembering the Spiritual Gifts

A Doorway to Truth (p. 52)

8.   Dreams offer so many treasures! You can highlight or underline the ones in this quote that appeal to you.

> *Dreams can show the future, the cause of illness, the reason for problems in a relationship, and more. Dreams are the last frontier.*
>
> *While dreams are a Mr. Fixit for someone who has learned how to interpret them, they have yet another side. They are a handy way to explore new realms of consciousness. . . .*
>
> *. . . A dream is simply a memory of a person's travels in the other planes, and they provide many experiences and insights to teach him how to run things better here.* (p. 52)

What's one gift you've received from your dreams this month? You can write it on this gift box.

Extra Writing Page
for this month's exercises and experiences

Extra Writing Page
for this month's exercises and experiences

"Earth is a school where Soul learns to become a Co-worker with God."

. . . God made earth a way station in time and space where people can unfold the qualities of love, compassion, and wisdom—traits available to all who have a strong desire for spiritual freedom. (p. 69)

4

Karma—
It All Comes
Back in the End

✳

*I*t's odd the way so many people dash through life and never stop to determine the reason for it.

In fact, ask some people why they bother to show up for work every day, and they would be at a loss to frame a suitable answer. ("Well, we've got to work.") And never mind looking for more than a reflex response to questions like, What is the meaning of life? What sort of God would curse so many infants with birth defects? Where does a Soul go when life is over?

In ECKANKAR, our name for the interplay of cause and effect in life is karma. In Judaism and Christianity, it is *sin*.

Paradise Lost

John Milton, in his epic poem *Paradise Lost*, tried to show the origin of the pain and suffering that dogs people from cradle to grave. He felt it started with Satan. The angel who led a rebellion of angels against God, Satan became an outcast, an enemy of all beings in heaven and on earth. But he got a chance to pass along his own misery—due to a separation from God—soon after God created Adam and Eve, parents of the human race.

His guile led them to disobey God.

From the first moment of disobedience, early humans had to deal with their own separation from God. So Milton had the characters in his epic flesh out his view of the war between the angels of light and darkness as they drove their war to the battlefield of earth.

Among the dark angels is Mammon, an angel who fell from grace through a reckless urge for material goods. His desire is to exploit nature and thus build a mighty empire on earth that will rival the splendors of heaven. Another ally of the dark forces is Belial, the angel whose advice to his fellows is to keep a low profile so God will forget them. It is a ploy to help reduce their suffering. Yet Belial opts for surrender to the vice of sloth instead of the will of God.

Among the other evil players is Sin. Daughter of Satan, she guards the gates of hell and gives him free access to the fields of earth below, where he can torment people at his pleasure. She and Death, her son, follow Satan to earth to accomplish their own selfish ends of destruction and fear.

Paradise Lost is a dramatic poem that captures the gist of people's relation to God in the Christian sense.

Karma or Sin?

Karma, like sin, is also a study about the origin of cause and effect, but it goes a step further. Karma offers an explanation for Soul's entry into a human body. Ask a Christian why God would bother to set people among the cats, dogs, horses, cattle, and other creatures of land, sea, and air; he would probably offer a helpless shrug.

"God's will is beyond human understanding," he might say.

Yet is it?

In ECKANKAR, most members would have a ready answer to that question: "Earth is a school where Soul learns to become a Co-worker with God."

That reply catches the true purpose of life. Earth is a school. God made earth a way station in time and space where people can unfold the qualities of love, compassion, and wisdom—traits available to all who have a strong desire for spiritual freedom. But perhaps the sharpest line of distinction we can draw between karma and sin is on the issue of time. The forgiveness of sin is available only during this lifetime. Get it now or perish.

That certainly is not the will of a loving God.

Sin—A Tool of Control

The idea of sin is a crude takeoff of spiritual law: It is a choke hold of a religion upon its people. It is a tool of control. Church leaders find a threat of punishment for sin a handy last resort to keep critics among their members in line—another way of saying, spiritually in the dark. The Christian Church of the Middle Ages has a vile record of brutality in curbing ideas that ran counter to its official dogma. The church did all within its power to keep Europe in the Dark Ages. Yet its most diligent efforts to block the work of scientists like Kepler, Brahe, and Galileo ended up in failure, in spite of the Inquisition.

The Christian church has a poor legacy as a champion for truth.

In fact, its history is one of suppression, for the Inquisition had the aid and blessing of the highest church authority, the pope, in carrying out the torture of its brightest minds. Those victims of the church never felt the gentle touch of mercy.

So what does ECKANKAR teach about karma?

Cycles of Karma

Karma is simply the law of action and reaction. The cycle of karma begins during a person's first incarnation, when the Lords of Karma place him or her (usually in a male body) into a setting that begins Soul's long journey in the material worlds. To start off, they give each person adi, or primal, karma. Unearned, it is a trait of either a positive or negative nature: bigotry, a spirit of grace, a miserly side, cruelty, lust, anger, or any other sign of a strong or weak character. Primal karma gets the individual into trouble. Like a stone dropped into a pond, his smallest act causes a series of ripples that rocks the karmic setting of family, tribe, or society. And a reaction occurs.

Should his primal karma be too much boldness, he might attack a tiger with his bare hands or challenge the chief for tribal leadership. If he were so lucky as to escape his folly, next time he would develop a better plan.

Let's say his primal karma is having too much sympathy. Others would soon take advantage of him until he found a way to balance it with a finer sense of discrimination. In short, he would learn to say no. There is a time and place for sympathy, yet given too freely, it exacts a toll in health and goodwill by holding one to the lower emotions.

Had the Lords of Karma given Soul a greedy nature in Its first incarnation, the forces of family and tribe would begin to wear it down as he tried to take undue advantage of them. He would be like the coyote in Native American lore: a trickster caught by his own tricks.

Thus primal karma is like the yeast that causes bread to rise, for it helps Soul get involved in the play of life.

It also develops the second stage of karma. Now the individual is much like a loose cannonball on a ship in rough seas, rolling back and forth, striking masts, crashing into walls, and bowling over people who happen to stand in the way. This second stage of karmic unfoldment is kriyaman, or daily, karma. By the hour, by the day, he adds to his ledger of karma, and also subtracts from it in the meantime. Unlike primal karma, the individual is responsible for all his daily karma and must someday repay it. He must balance the books. Until then, he often thinks he is free to juggle them at will.

The third type of karma is prarabdh karma, also fate karma, or destiny. At the close of Soul's first incarnation, and each after that, the Lords of Karma study Soul's record of accounts and pass a verdict of judgment. Their verdict forms the basis for Soul's next incarnation. It is a sum of all good karma minus the negative deeds, and in the end, it is the individual's karmic record that sets the conditions for the next life. Male or female? Will the person come into a rich or poor, material or spiritual family? Will the individual be comely or not?

All depends upon fate. Yet fate, or destiny, is merely a personal creation made by a lifetime of choices.

The fourth level of karma is sinchit karma. Also known as reserve karma, it is a surplus of credits and debits of past lives, like a savings account in a bank. The Lords of Karma sometimes draw upon this karma. When an individual gets ahead in his present life and has a handle upon the conditions imposed by his fate karma, the Lords of Karma hand him some credits or debits from his past.

There is a way to tell when a person draws upon reserve karma. All his or her life, an individual will fit into a steady lifestyle of some sort, but suddenly finds a brand-new life.

Often it is someone who wins a lottery. People who don't understand the workings of karma write off such good fortune as fool's luck. But the winner has earned the money. Another person may have misfortune, yet he, too, is cleaning up his accounts for this present life—paying a debt from the past. Sooner or later, an individual needs to square his record of karma. He needs to balance his karmic books, either in this lifetime or in another.

An ECKist who is aware of the exact nature of the Law of Karma can sidestep the shadow of envy that often engulfs those who do not understand the sudden good fortune of others. All is in its rightful place. Everything is at the exact station it deserves in life, so he can get on with his own unfoldment and keep a cheerful spirit.

What Karma Brings Us

What do you gain by your karma?

"If the karma of man has brought him nothing more than a capacity to love, then he has not lived in vain for a thousand past lives." So says *The Shariyat-Ki-Sugmad*, Book Two.

ECK Masters like Rebazar Tarzs, Fubbi Quantz, and Yaubl Sacabi are all Co-workers with God, having served their terms as apprentices on the path of ECK. Like you and every student of ECK, they once had to deal with their spiritual credits and debts too. In the end, they triumphed over the base desires common to mankind. Now they live in God Consciousness.

The Shariyat adds: "Those who live in the heavenly

worlds enjoy the presence of the Mahanta, the Living ECK Master for he dwells on all planes in the bodies furnished him by the SUGMAD. They drink the nectar of immortality; and death, karma, and all pain are entirely absent in these worlds."

But this leads to a question. Where do the believers in the theory of sin go at death in contrast to those who know about the Law of Karma?

It is not belief or knowledge that decides a person's place in the next life, whether it be on earth or some higher plane of God. The gauge is one's thought and action. How did he or she behave in the last life? The Lords of Karma judge the merit of an individual's deeds and not his intent, nor is there any allowance for wrong beliefs in the form of plea bargaining. A believer and nonbeliever are judged alike—by the merits of their case. The Christian belief about the Judgment Day is about reward and punishment. Yet that is not so. Each person receives an absolutely fair and impartial hearing in the Court of Karma, and the sentence is just.

However, the Mahanta takes his chelas directly to the place they have earned. Thus, an ECK chela will never go before the Lords of Karma.

Charles Darwin, the English naturalist, said in a letter to Henry Fawcett in 1861, "All observation must be for or against some view if it is to be of any service!"

So let's look at the contrast between sin and karma with that in mind.

Soul Gaining Experience

The theory of sin claims that Soul lives but once in the human form. All people are born in sin and face eternal damnation, unless they repent of their sins in this lifetime.

At death, a person's Soul goes either to heaven or hell, or, in some cases, to a purgatory. In the end, a savior takes on the responsibility for a person's deeds, not the person himself. Yet what is the reason for birth? Does chance cause one's birth to occur in a Christian family, where baptism (the key to salvation) is automatic for many infants? Then what of free will?

There is no allowance for people before the birth of Christ, nor for those who never had the opportunity to hear the Christian gospel.

Their fate is uncertain.

The works of ECK teach the Law of Karma. God sent each Soul into the lower worlds to gain experience, someday to become a Co-worker with God. Soul goes on a long journey into the material worlds over many lifetimes, where It gains more love, wisdom, and understanding each time. The way to spiritual freedom is to find the Mahanta, the Living ECK Master. He is the Wayshower. Each person must answer for all deeds, for he knows the Law of Karma requires him to balance the accounts of Soul.

Soul Travel allows a member of ECK to explore the heavens of God before the death of this human shell.

Each experience, on earth or in the other worlds, adds to a Soul's ability to love and serve God. At death, an ECK chela will bypass the Court of Judgment, for the Mahanta takes him or her directly to a new home in the heaven they have earned.

Finally, Soul exists because God loves It.

And Soul is eternal.

This Month's Exercise

Your spiritual exercise for this month keys in on the word *mana* (chanted as mah-NAY or mah-NAH). It is the word to chant for the Causal Plane, the place of storage for your karmic records.

Sing this word silently or aloud. Be in a quiet room where no one will disturb you for twenty minutes to half an hour. Clear your mind of all thoughts. Chant the word until you feel like stopping, then sit in silence for the rest of the twenty- to thirty-minute session.

Gently keep your attention upon the top of your head. That is the crown chakra. It is the place where Soul finds the easiest bridge to the other worlds via Soul Travel. Keep your eye of imagination open for any appearance of Light or Sound, for that will be the ECK—the Holy Spirit or Voice of God—reaching out to give you Its divine love.

In some way, inwardly or outwardly, the ECK will open your awareness to the place of karma in your spiritual life.

There is nothing to worry about, for holy people have used this method and similar ones for centuries to reach God.

Keep a small journal of any sights, sounds, or impressions during your spiritual exercise. Date each entry.

Workbook Activities

1.   *"Earth is a school where Soul learns to become a Co-worker with God."*

    That reply catches the true purpose of life. Earth is a school. God made earth a way station in time and space where people can unfold the qualities of love, compassion, and wisdom—traits available to all who have a strong desire for spiritual freedom.
(p. 69)

Imagine you're in a special classroom and the topic for today is fascinating: the Law of Karma. As you read this lesson, what insights stand out to help you live life with more love, compassion, and wisdom?

The Spiritual exercise for this month is to Soul Travel to the Causal Plane. You'll find out how on pages 74–75.

2.   *But perhaps the sharpest line of distinction we*
        can draw between karma and sin is on the issue of
        time. (p. 69)

Choose an event in the news or something you've heard about that caught your attention. Consider it as an example of karma. Does this viewpoint bring more understanding to the issue? What insights come to you?

Cycles of Karma (pp. 70–72)

3.   *Thus primal karma is like the yeast that causes
             bread to rise, for it helps Soul get involved in the
             play of life.* (p. 71)

Let's have some fun with the four types of karma
that are described on pages 70–72. They explain
the play of life.

Can you think of something from a game or sport
that illustrates one of the types of karma listed
below? (For example, many board games begin
with a roll of the dice. This gets you started in the
game, just as primal karma gets you started in the
play of life.)

You can choose from:

Primal karma

Daily karma

Fate karma

Reserve karma

4.　　　*Sooner or later, an individual needs to square his record of karma. He needs to balance his karmic books, either in this lifetime or in another.* (p. 72)

🎧 Audio Excerpt 5

You can hear more about the Law of Karma in this excerpt from the talk "The Law of Returns."

Ask the Mahanta, the Inner Master, to show you a recent example of daily karma in your life: how something you did caused a certain outcome.

What insights come to you? How did this experience give you more spiritual freedom?

What Karma Brings Us (pp. 72–73)

5.   *What do you gain by your karma?*
       "If the karma of man has brought him nothing
       more than a capacity to love, then he has not lived
       in vain for a thousand past lives." (p. 72)

Let's explore some gifts of karma. Choose a
challenge in your life, and jot it below.

Now write down a blessing in your life.

How do these relate to karma? To gaining more
divine love? You can write your insights here.

Soul Gaining Experience (pp. 73–74)

6. One of the most important messages of ECK is in this discourse. Imagine the Mahanta, the Inner Master, saying the following words to you:

    Soul exists because God loves It. (p. 74)

    Take a moment to ask the Mahanta, the Inner Master, for more understanding of this key principle, this heartsong of ECK. Then listen for the Mahanta's response—just for you. What do you perceive? You can note your experience below.

This Month's Exercise
A technique for Soul Travel to the Causal Plane,
pp. 74–75

7.   *Your spiritual exercise for this month keys in
on the word* mana *(chanted as mah-NAY or
mah-NAH). It is the word to chant for the
Causal Plane, the place of storage for your
karmic records. . . .*

   *Keep a small journal of any sights, sounds,
or impressions during your spiritual exercise.
Date each entry.* (pp. 74–75)

As you do your daily spiritual exercise, you
can write your experiences here or in your
journal. Use the extra writing pages (pp. 84–
85) if you need more space.

Date   Sights, sounds, impressions

Spotlight on ECK
Noticing and Remembering the Spiritual Gifts

8.   *In some way, inwardly or outwardly, the ECK will open your awareness to the place of karma in your spiritual life.* (p. 75)

You may find it enlightening to look over your journal entries at the end of the month. What's one change you've noticed in yourself because of this discourse lesson?

Extra Writing Page
for this month's exercises and experiences

Extra Writing Page
for this month's exercises and experiences

If you accept reincarnation, you are likely to be a more self-reliant and responsible person. How could you not be? (p. 93)

5

Reincarnation— Why You Came to Earth Again

✳

*E*arly during my own study of ECKANKAR, Paul Twitchell used to drop hints about certain truths that usually caught me and others by surprise.

Once he told a chela, a student of ECK, that he was not a reincarnation of Saint Paul, the apostle. A rumor said he was. On another occasion, he went to Greece with his wife, Gail. There he spoke of the problems he'd made for himself in a past life because of his desire to learn some new side of God. The past was very real to him. He knew that rebirth into another human body is a fact of life, and he tried to pass his understanding on to the chelas of ECK.

So the issue is, Many lives or just one?

Our beliefs make us different. Often people in Western countries hold to a one-life theory due to the influence of the Christian church. That theory makes for a lot of problems. It has no clear-cut answer for many cases where injustice appears to occur: deformed babies, the deaths of youth in their prime, injury, accidents, failed marriages, ill health, poverty, and other unhappy states.

A serious shortcoming of Christianity has been its failure to teach the laws of karma and reincarnation. This blind spot has held people back spiritually, and it is simply because their leaders do not know these divine laws. So priests, rabbis, ministers, and others spread false doctrine by their adamant denial of reincarnation.

What, then, is the truth?

Soul is eternal. It has no beginning or end. And It exists because God loves It. Keep these three principles in your heart and mind, because they are key to the tenets of reincarnation.

Cycle of Rebirth

How did the cycle of rebirth start? Souls were playing in heaven when SUGMAD (God) saw their lack of experience. Then the Voice of God—the ECK, Holy Spirit—went forth to create the worlds of matter, energy, time, and space. The two main aspects of ECK are Sound and Light. The action of these two divine elements drew off a dividing line from the pure regions of Sound and Light, the spiritual worlds, and brought into being the gases, liquids, and solids. From these, the ECK fashioned a variety of planes, galaxies, stars, planets, and creatures.

In very simple terms, creation formed structure. It was nothing less than the ordering of matter and energy in space and time. And so these lower universes came to be.

God's plan was to build a special garden in which Souls could develop the divine qualities that had seen neglect during Souls' carefree play in heaven. The result was the planes of the lower order: the Etheric, Mental, Causal, Astral, and Physical. You—as Soul, the image of God's Light and Sound—will sometime pass through each of these planes, in a multitude of bodies, to experience the full range of life.

In the end, you become a Co-worker with God.

Becoming a Co-worker with God

Each who reaches that high level of service to life is able and willing to serve beings on every plane of existence with the divine qualities of love, wisdom, joy, and compassion.

A Co-worker is a Soul at play. But now Its play has purpose, which it lacked before Soul began Its long stint in the university of life: taking on and shedding human bodies under the exact and just codes of divine law. People may accept or reject the challenge of finding their true place in life. It's up to them. A person may spend entire lifetimes in pursuit of a certain passion, such as the quest for knowledge or power, simply because he must have every experience to develop a pure heart.

I recall many of my own past lives. Of course, this recollection is largely of those lives with special meaning for the present one, for you and everyone else has many thousands of lives to his credit in the lower worlds. Later in this discourse there will be a spiritual exercise to start research into your own past, should you wish to do so.

Learning about Ourselves

My own past lives have run the gamut of experience. They include lives in both a male and female form, as a noble, a peasant, a healer, the equivalent of a prime minister, a knight, and a slave. Sometimes it was even as a soldier, a worker with mosaic design, or a rug merchant.

Enemies put me to the sword. In a later lifetime, I was

quick to repay the favor. Later still, my adversaries had another chance to even the score, which they did with pleasure. Finally, the pattern got old. When we began to wear down, we looked for a better place and time in which to take on a human body again. We wanted a better set of conditions, where we might also have a chance to learn each other's virtues.

In doing so, we learned about ourselves.

A study of the distant past is a highly interesting pursuit for some. It can reveal the reason for our likes and dislikes, bring to light the secret behind friendships and enmities, and reveal mental grooves and opinions that keep us in a state of misery.

In passing, I need to explain a phrase used by Paul Twitchell: "Cease to cherish opinions." ECK initiates may misunderstand his intent. They may think it means to have no opinions at all, so they cheat themselves out of many rich experiences in life. They have a fear of joining groups with social or political agendas, for they feel it is acting out opinions, a practice they feel is wrong in ECKANKAR. This phrase is like the misconception that many have about this biblical quote from Saint Paul: "For the love of money is the root of all evil."

They leave off "For the love of."

ECKists can and do have opinions, for opinions are a part of living. Paul Twitchell did not say, "Cease to have opinions." Just cease to *cherish* them.

Mental Grooves

It is the mental grooves, or attitudes, which people cherish that hold them back in life and cause most of their unhappiness and misery. Often the cause lies in a past life. For example, a person trying to cope with the hazards of vanity might appear stubborn to others, given to endless argument. He has set too high a value upon his own opinions. When he forces his will upon others by a firm refusal to compromise, they make him pay the price in some way later.

A stubborn man might anger his superior or those who work under him. So sure his opinion is right, he cuts off others in midsentence. But he will pay. Someone will eventually get him back; it's only a question of time.

The people we meet at work, in ECK Satsang classes, in the community, and especially in our own families are no passing strangers—people dropped into our sphere by some divine whim or joke. They helped us develop into what we are today, while we in turn helped them. Our worst enemies and closest friends from our past lives are among our acquaintances, a fact which explains why we often feel at home so quickly in a new town, school, or place of employment. We know those people, and they know us. Hardly any of the memories are conscious, of course, yet they are there. They take form in how we have an immediate liking or dislike for some people we've just met for the first time in this life.

People have individual tastes in their migrations. For example, some people return to earth and rejoin a tight family circle: a departed person comes back to be his own grandson, or a woman becomes her own niece. Such returns are common. Others go far afield, joining groups merely for the adventure of it.

Look at your own family sometime. You are likely to see newborn babies among your relatives who act an awful lot like someone you once knew well but who passed on. The baby will have an expression that tells of a lifetime of living. All that in the face of a newborn. You will often see a baby with a strong attraction for a certain member of the family, a sign that a strong bond of love was once between them.

But most people never notice.

The Logic of Reincarnation

Reincarnation makes sense if only from a logical point of view. It says a lot about the unexplained loves and hates of people. Whether or not people choose to believe in rebirth, they rub shoulders with it every day. There is no running from it.

Even animals follow the cycle of return, often coming back to the same owner or place repeatedly. People in their supreme vanity are likely to feel they are God's highest creation, well above the likes of dogs, cats, pigs, and chickens. But Soul is Soul. A particular Soul may choose to exist at that level of incarnation, which does not make it a lesser creation. Everything has a place in life, otherwise it would not exist.

Even as the Christian church had to accept the sun, and not the earth, as the center of our planetary system, so the church must continue to bend the knee to truth. In time, it will be clear even to the church that life exists on other planets.

The point is that earth, as well as the physical universe, is a vast garden to educate Souls. Though the Christian church was not aware of people in the Americas before the voyages of Columbus, many hundreds of thousands living there got along very well indeed without a papal blessing. The Souls who inhabited the bodies of the Native Americans were also under the laws of karma and reincarnation. They clashed in war, worshipped their gods, and loved their dear ones just like people in other parts of the world.

Peace to a Troubled Heart

The knowledge and acceptance of rebirth can bring peace to many a troubled heart.

When our loved ones leave us at death, we can take comfort that we shall meet again—and often, very soon. This knowledge can give us a more even disposition. In the face of trouble and hardship, we know that the worst that life can dish out to us always adds to some spiritual good.

It is not our intent here to prove reincarnation with a list of case histories. Most libraries and bookstores have plenty of material on that, because people today, especially those who are ready for ECKANKAR, have already realized the truth of reincarnation on their own. All I want to point out now is that a belief in rebirth makes you different from the average person around you. Unless, of course, you happen to live in India or some other region that teaches it as part of a particular religion, like Hinduism.

You Become More Self-Reliant

If you accept reincarnation, you are likely to be a more self-reliant and responsible person. How could you not be?

At death, Soul leaves the body. You are Soul, the true identity of the person that the orthodox church is still trying to identify. The church speaks of "your soul," which implies a possession that *you* own. Who then are *you* in such a cosmology—a Soul that has a soul? Why speak of someone having a soul, unless the speaker has no idea about truth and its nature: that Soul takes on a human body at birth and leaves it at death. The human body is the possession. It is not the other way around.

A simple truth like this is beyond the ability of the

orthodox church to handle, and that, unfortunately, is at the root of all the false teachings of the church about the nature of Soul. We won't go into the issue of abortion here.

Overcome Fear of Death

Most people have a terrible fear of death due to the instinct for survival so deeply embedded in them, which is only right. The fear comes of having to face their attachments to this world. They may include mate, family, possessions, and even their thoughts, which they believe to be the core of what makes them a person. So when death comes, they are afraid to leave the things of this life behind, because they feel they risk extinction. But as Soul begins to gather Itself together and take leave of the body, It expands into a higher state of being: the Astral.

In that moment, the individual is free. It is an experience he or she has had so often in the past, but has forgotten until this moment of departure from another life on earth. All feels natural. Indeed, all is well. A loved one meets the individual on the other side to guide him to his new home in the other worlds, which for most people is on the Astral Plane.

At death, the Mahanta meets the ECK chela. The Master takes him directly to the place he has earned, bypassing the Dharam Raya, the judge of those who leave the physical plane.

Then the individual, ECKist or otherwise, gets a briefing on credits earned or missed in the past life. A course of remedial study then prepares him or her for a new life on earth or in some other place, depending upon the karma due. He accepts this instruction gladly.

This Month's Exercise

The Spiritual Exercise of ECK for this month is to help you glimpse a past life or two. It goes as follows:

The word to chant is *mana* again, the word from the Causal Plane that you used last month. Only this time, sing it in groups of three: "Mana . . . mana . . . mana (chanted as mah-NAY or mah-NAH)." Sing it aloud three times, then silently three more times. Repeat this pattern for ten minutes or so, when the Mahanta will prompt you to stop chanting and sit in silence.

Then gently watch the screen of your mind and listen. It will take persistence to see a past life, but it can be done. It may come during contemplation, or later in a dream. Be patient. Keep your face toward the Light and Sound of God.

Workbook Activities

1.   *Early during my own study of ECKANKAR, Paul Twitchell used to drop hints about certain truths that usually caught me and others by surprise.* (p. 87)

This lesson begins with some hints about certain truths from Paul Twitchell, the modern-day founder of ECKANKAR. And you'll find more hints about truth throughout this discourse. Want to uncover some? As you read this lesson, what catches you by surprise or stands out for you? Use the extra writing page (p. 103) if you need more space.

2.   Here are some key principles of ECK:

> *Soul is eternal. It has no beginning or end.*
> *And It exists because God loves It. Keep these three*
> *principles in your heart and mind, because they are*
> *key to the tenets of reincarnation.* (p. 88)

These principles are describing *you*. Want to explore them a little more? Ask the Mahanta, the Inner Master, to show you how these principles can unlock the secrets of reincarnation. Record your experience here.

 This month's spiritual exercise gives step-by-step guidance on how to glimpse a past life. See page 95.

Mental Grooves (pp. 90–92)

3. If you wish, take a quick look at something that has caused you unhappiness lately. Then read the following quote.

    It is the mental grooves, or attitudes, which people cherish that hold them back in life and cause most of their unhappiness and misery. Often the cause lies in a past life. (p. 90)

    You can write a brief note asking the Mahanta, the Inner Master, to show you the cause of your unhappiness.

    Dear Mahanta,

    Watch for the Mahanta's reply—just for you. What do you perceive?

4.   *The people we meet at work, in ECK Satsang classes, in the community, and especially in our own families are no passing strangers—people dropped into our sphere by some divine whim or joke. They helped us develop into what we are today, while we in turn helped them. Our worst enemies and closest friends from our past lives are among our acquaintances.* (p. 91)

Here's a way to look for past-life connections with those in your life today. Write down the names of two people you know today who you might have known in a past life.

Then, next to each name, jot down how this person helped you to develop into who and what you are today.

Names   How you were helped

1)

2)

Peace to a Troubled Heart (p. 93)

5. *It is not our intent here to prove reincarnation with a list of case histories. Most libraries and bookstores have plenty of material on that, because people today, especially those who are ready for ECKANKAR, have already realized the truth of reincarnation on their own.* (p. 93)

Take a moment to reflect: When did the idea of reincarnation first become true for you? What happened to cause this?

6. As you read the following quote, what benefits of reincarnation appeal to you? You can highlight or underline them.

> *The knowledge and acceptance of rebirth can bring peace to many a troubled heart.*
> *When our loved ones leave us at death, we can take comfort that we shall meet again—and often, very soon. This knowledge can give us a more even disposition. In the face of trouble and hardship, we know that the worst that life can dish out to us always adds to some spiritual good.* (p. 93)

Has the knowledge of reincarnation brought understanding or other benefits to you? Maybe in the face of a loss, injustice, or hardship? You can note your experiences here.

This Month's Exercise

A technique to glimpse a past life, p. 95

7. Ready to do some past-life exploring? The spiritual exercise for this month is found on page 95. It offers specific guidance to help you get a glimpse of a past life. As you read the quote below, you can highlight or underline the steps of this spiritual exercise.

> *The word to chant is* mana *again, the word from the Causal Plane that you used last month. Only this time, sing it in groups of three: "Mana . . . mana . . . mana (chanted as mah-NAY or mah-NAH)." Sing it aloud three times, then silently three more times. Repeat this pattern for ten minutes or so, when the Mahanta will prompt you to stop chanting and sit in silence.*
> *Then gently watch the screen of your mind and listen.* (p. 95)

You can record your experiences here, in your journal, or on p. 103. Draw a star by one past life that came to you in a contemplation or in a dream.

Spotlight on ECK
Noticing and Remembering the Spiritual Gifts

8.   *It will take persistence to see a past life, but it can be done. It may come during contemplation, or later in a dream. Be patient. Keep your face toward the Light and Sound of God.* (p. 95)

Audio Excerpt 6

You can hear how *The Easy Way Discourses* helped a new ECKist recognize some of her past lives in this excerpt from the talk "God's Love Is a Wonderful Thing."

How did you recognize your past-life experiences? Did you just know? Or did you have a dream or image of another country? Maybe another time period?

You can note any tips for recognizing past lives here. You may want to try them in the future.

Extra Writing Page
for this month's exercises and experiences

Your first is the Dream Initiation. The Mahanta, the Dream Master, comes in a dream to give you an experience or insight that acts like a seed for spiritual growth. But mainly, he comes to connect you with the Sound Current. (p. 106)

6

Your
Initiations in ECK

✴

The ECK initiations are your key to a richer and more abundant life. Many hundreds of words speak about them in the ECK works, but until the Mahanta begins to open your Spiritual Eye at the First Initiation, all those words will only be words.

What exactly is an ECK initiation?

It is the most holy sacrament in ECKANKAR, which links you directly with the Light and Sound of God. It is also the first step to spiritual freedom.

The ECK initiation begins to open your heart to love, because love is the mainstay of life and, so also, the foundation of the ECK teachings. In fact, ECK (Divine Spirit) is love. It is life. You are Soul, and in the highest spiritual state you share in all the divine qualities of God: love, wisdom, and power.

The Shariyat-Ki-Sugmad, Book One, says:

> The three attributes derived from Soul's
> relationship with God are love, wisdom, and

power. Of these three, the greatest is love. Man understands this more than he does the other attributes. Reality has but one attribute and that is love. All love is given to Soul when It is linked with the ECK, the Audible Life Stream.

Doorway to a New Life

What, then, is the ECK initiation? It is your doorway to life, love, and truth.

During my early days in ECKANKAR, I must say that the ECK initiations meant very little to me. Others have said the same. But as time passed, most of us saw our interest, awareness, and joy in the details and events of everyday life begin to grow. The Mahanta, by the ECK initiation, had started us on our way home to God. And we were finally aware of it.

At each initiation, from your first to the highest, the Mahanta greets you in some region of the worlds of God, making a more direct link between you and the ECK. He opens your vision and your heart. And after each of these holy occasions, outer or inner, you must take the spiritual gifts of SUGMAD and do something better with your life. The rite of initiation is more than a passive act. Unlike baptism, the basis for the ECK initiations is the Sound and Light of God, which, you must know by now, are the Voice of God in the purest form.

Two Parts of Initiation

Each ECK initiation, except the first, is in two parts. Your first is the Dream Initiation. The Mahanta, the Dream Master, comes in a dream to give you an experience or insight that acts like a seed for spiritual growth. But mainly, he comes to connect you with the Sound Current.

106

The Shariyat, Book Two, says:

> The initiation for the seeker of God on the path of Eckankar is the gateway into the mysteries of the Sugmad. It is through the rites of initiation that the uninitiated gains deliverance from the lower self and enters into the worlds of freedom and immortality.

Shed Your Karmic Load

The ECK initiation is the culmination and fulfillment of karma and reincarnation, the two stern teachers of Souls in the lower worlds. Each person here grapples with the five deceptions of the mind. Most ECK chelas are all too familiar with them: lust, anger, greed, attachment, and vanity. They are a part of the primal karma of every individual, the burden every Soul carries while in the regions of matter, energy, space, and time—until he meets the Mahanta, the Living ECK Master.

The Master, by initiation, helps each chela shed the load. In the end, the trickery of the mind loses the long bout for control, and Soul is ready to start on the journey home to God.

The following story shows how the passions drive each Soul. They cause Soul to act (to make daily karma) and thus gain the spiritual experience that weakens the grasp of the five passions of the mind. Finally, that person is ready to meet the Mahanta again. Then the journey to God begins.

The Chase of Life

The chase started in a ghetto. Michael stood in a crowd of young men watching a black brother climb into an old car and back it down a steep, grassy incline at a perilous angle.

The car overturned. There were no injuries, except to

the pride of the crowd. It shamed them to have an outsider see the stupidity of one of their own. The outsider was white. He rushed up to help the other bystanders remove the driver and his passenger from the car. Both were shaken, but both emerged unscathed.

Because of shame, as stated above, the mood of the crowd now turned sour.

The lone white person on the scene was the Mahanta, the Living ECK Master, there in his role as agent for God. Faster than he could run for it, the crowd did a change of behavior: from watchers of a neutral scene to actors in a play of malice. In short, the crowd became a mob. It turned its fury upon the Mahanta, first with angry shouts of, "What you doing here, Whitey?" Then with threats: "I'll bust your bones."

Among those with the loudest shouts of this sort of insanity was Michael, who reached into the trunk of the car and brought out a short length of chain. Sneering, he wrapped it around his fist.

"I want to talk to you, Whitey."

The chase began.

Michael and others in the mob turned their blind, mad fury upon the Mahanta, rushing at him with murder in mind. Wah Z turned to run. Runners in the mob jostled each other, trying to get in the most direct line behind him, each wanting to be first to land a blow.

Near the ghetto lay brush and a swamp. Wah Z, cut off from an escape to the left or right by faster runners, ran directly into the briar patch like a rabbit. Many of his pursuers, crowded by runners on either side, fell off the narrow path he took through the briars and thus felt the sharp bite of thorns. Pain and sweat were not part of their lifestyle, so the laziest in the mob quit the race.

Anyway, Michael would catch and beat this whitey.

The Mahanta ran on. He led the chase from the Astral Plane, where it had begun, to the Physical Plane, with Michael just a few short steps behind him. In life after life, Michael kept up the chase. He unleashed his anger at all who got between him and his quarry, striking them as he would the Mahanta. Cursing them as he would the Mahanta. Wishing them evil, as he did the Mahanta. And all the while, thinking he was in the right.

But then the Master changed the rules. The chase had begun, Michael liked to think, with himself in charge. The Mahanta was only a scared weakling. Yet he had an annoying way of keeping in the lead, just out of Michael's reach.

Wah Z had run inside a building. A cruel smile lit Michael's face: He'd trapped the quarry. The entrance led into a circular room with many doors, but Michael headed right for the one that had just slammed. However, it led into a second round chamber, ringed by more doors. Which had Whitey taken? Opening each door in turn, Michael found that each led to a white circular room, the same as the one he stood in now. The Mahanta had left; Michael had lost his trail.

Still full of hate and anger, Michael decided to try one door after another, for surely the chase would end behind one of the doors. Every sense alert, he began to watch and listen for anything unusual.

Hopelessly lost, each sterile white room he entered now changed in character: a single large mural graced the circular wall and came to life.

Indeed, it *was* life.

Each picture was a lifetime—once in Egypt, then in Spain, in Switzerland, in France, England, Norway, Germany, and the Americas. But he also put in decades of living in Asia, in the Antarctic before it grew cold, and in Australia. Always in the back of his mind was his quest for the Mahanta.

In each life, Michael ran into many more briars and brambles, still at a fast pace, thus feeling every sting and bite of hate and anger prick his own skin. But in time, his pace slackened. As it did, he found himself more at peace inside. The awful emotions of hate, anger, lust, and a few others he had noticed during the chase began to subside. They caused too much pain.

As the chase changed, so did Michael's face. Once hard, cut by deep lines, his face now often wore a look of amusement, warmth, laughter, and even compassion.

One day, quite unaware of it, Michael stopped the chase.

It was on that very day that the Mahanta, the Living ECK Master stepped into sight again, for the first time in ages. Michael had forgotten him. When this person, this stranger, called him by name, Michael felt a stab of wild terror in his chest. He began to run. But his legs simply refused to hold their ground. Time had run his hourglass empty of sand, of hate, of the will to do violence to any of God's creatures. So what could account for this sudden fear of a pleasant fellow calling him by name?

"You've changed, Michael," he called. "Look at yourself. Do you know who you are?"

Of course, he knew—he was Michael.

The stranger smiled and said, "Yes, Michael, you are Soul."

Soul.

Michael knew about soul brothers and soul food, but Soul? There was a clear ring to the word, different in any sense than he had ever used. Soul. A good sound. There was music to the word.

The Master took him by the arm and turned him around. A lofty mountain rose before them. "The mountain of God," said the Mahanta. "It's a long, hard climb to the top, but from there you can see forever."

And so Michael's chase had ended, as his climb to God began.

Soul Wants Truth

The story of Michael is that of every man, woman, and child—for Soul has no race, creed, color, gender, or religion. Nothing may lay claim to It, for Soul is of God. The story of Soul in the lower worlds is the quest for spiritual freedom, for Soul here has long forgotten Its unique relationship with God and is a slave to the mind.

People say they want truth; indeed, many already claim to have it. Yet in the next breath they complain about injustice, are unhappy, show greed, temper, or ill will. Nor does it end there with such self-proclaimed models of truth.

They also give in to gluttony or excessive drink, are stingy, put on airs, and have a greater use for material goods than for spiritual gifts. They are like Michael in the parable above. Like Michael, they have a dim awareness of wrongs they've done to others in past lives in the name of God, humanity, and religion.

But what do they fear?

The mirror of Soul is but a reflection of truth, so the images in the mirror are simply your own. In ECK, there is no eternal death. The love of God is perfect in justice, and every Soul will eventually return to the Ocean of Love and Mercy. No evil is so bad that it cannot be undone.

A Secret Rite

What can you expect in the ECK initiation?

The Mahanta opens each person to the Sound and Light of God during the initiation, but some people simply do not recall the occasion. They do sense a change in their spiritual state, though they cannot point to the direction of change. Yet the initiation is holy and true. By this secret rite (only so because it comes to you alone on the inner planes), you move into a higher level of fellowship with others who hold spiritual values much like your own.

The Mahanta, the Living ECK Master gives the ECK initiation. Agent of SUGMAD, he is the channel by which the love, wisdom, and power of that initiation level reach the individual, for the spiritual power flows from him. Someday, all beings must come to ECK if they would move into the high worlds of God.

Some would argue this point, but it remains beyond dispute.

The Mahanta, the Living ECK Master chooses a group of trusted initiates to serve in the capacity of Initiator, to give many of the outer initiations in his stead. Yet they are only channels for the Mahanta, who gives them the spiritual power to pass the secret word, or mantra, to the person to use for protection and upliftment. The First Initiation is a purely inner rite. The Dream Master, the Mahanta, gives it to the individual in the dream state sometime during the first year of ECK study.

The Second Initiation comes after two years of study. It has two parts—both an inner and outer rite—as do all the ECK initiations up to and including the Eighth Circle.

The ECK Initiator acts out a role of high service to ECK in being a channel for an initiation. The Mahanta drives home to each Initiator the love and beauty of each such occasion and asks them to be clean in body, mind, and Soul. So the Initiator also finds it helpful to do a spiritual exercise before giving an initiation in the name of the Mahanta.

In short, the real purpose of the ECK initiation is to give each person a greater love for God.

This Month's Exercise

The spiritual exercise this month is to open your heart to a greater love for God and so make you ready for an ECK initiation in the future.

This technique works for all circles of initiation. There are many initiations that occur on the inner planes between the outer ones, which mark a major step in unfoldment. So for this exercise, you are to read a chapter from *Stranger by the River* by Paul Twitchell. You will find it most helpful.

Before you do your spiritual exercises this month, I ask you to read chapter 23, "The Trembling of a Star." It deals with the ECK initiation in a beautiful and memorable way, a reminder to each of the Star of God. There you will learn what the ECK initiation means in clear and simple terms. Read this chapter often. You will find it a source of spiritual food and drink, a sure refreshment for the needs of Soul.

Contemplate upon this chapter for fifteen minutes to half an hour. Chant *HU* as usual.

Workbook Activities

1.   *What exactly is an ECK initiation?*
    It is the most holy sacrament in ECKANKAR,
which links you directly with the Light and Sound
of God. It is also the first step to spiritual freedom.
(p. 105)

Do you have any questions about the ECK initiation, such as, What is it? What happens? And how
will it help me spiritually? You can write them
here.

As you read this lesson, you can highlight or
underline the answers that you discover.

Want to prepare for a future initiation? This
month's spiritual exercise shows how to open
your heart using the book *Stranger by the River* by
Paul Twitchell. See details on page 113.

2.   *The ECK initiation begins to open your heart to*
          love, because love is the mainstay of life and, so
          also, the foundation of the ECK teachings. In fact,
          ECK (Divine Spirit) is love. It is life. You are Soul,
          and in the highest spiritual state you share in all
          the divine qualities of God: love, wisdom, and
          power. (p. 105)

     Is there a sentence in this discourse that especially
     inspires you—that opens your heart to a greater
     love for God? You can write it here, along with
     your thoughts or feelings about it.

Doorway to a New Life (p. 106)

3.   *During my early days in ECKANKAR, I must
say that the ECK initiations meant very little to me.
Others have said the same. But as time passed, most
of us saw our interest, awareness, and joy in the
details and events of everyday life begin to grow.
The Mahanta, by the ECK initiation, had started us
on our way home to God. And we were finally
aware of it.* (p. 106)

Step back for a few minutes, and take a look at
your life during the past week. Does something
shine for you or stand out from the routine of
your day? It could be a small thing that caught
your interest, made you smile, or brought an
insight. You can record it here as a marker on
your way home to God.

The Chase of Life (pp. 107–11)

4.   *The following story shows how the passions drive
         each Soul. They cause Soul to act (to make daily
         karma) and thus gain the spiritual experience that
         weakens the grasp of the five passions of the mind.
         Finally, that person is ready to meet the Mahanta
         again. Then the journey to God begins.* (p. 107)

Ready for some adventure? Imagine you're watching a movie as you read "The Chase of Life" on
pages 107–11. Then have a conversation with the
Mahanta, the Inner Master, and explore Michael's
story together.

For example, you may wonder what part anger
played in helping Michael on his journey home to
God. And how does Michael's story relate to your
life today? If you wish, you can note your insights
here.

5.   The following quote is from the end of Michael's
     story:

>   *The Master took him by the arm and turned*
>   *him around. A lofty mountain rose before them.*
>   *"The mountain of God," said the Mahanta. "It's a*
>   *long, hard climb to the top, but from there you can*
>   *see forever."*
>   *And so Michael's chase had ended, as his climb*
>   *to God began.* (p. 111)

Imagine you're standing with Wah Z (my spiritual
name) as I show you the mountain of God. You
can draw a rough sketch of this mountain in the
space below.

If you wish, you can add a sketch (even stick
figures) of Wah Z and yourself, standing in front
of the mountain.

What are you feeling at this moment? What is
Wah Z saying or doing?

A Secret Rite (pp. 112–13)

6. *The First Initiation is a purely inner rite. The Dream Master, the Mahanta, gives it to the individual in the dream state sometime during the first year of ECK study.* (p. 112)

🎧 **Audio Excerpt 7**

Would you like a preview of the initiation experience? In this excerpt from the talk "The Rope of Karma," you can listen to a description of what happens during an ECK initiation. Note below any insights that come to you.

✎

You may want to watch for an inner initiation in the coming months. It can come as a special dream or a new awareness that you have upon awakening. Some have found it helpful to keep a dream journal. It can be a simple notebook to record your dreams and insights as you wake up.

7. The spiritual exercise for this month involves reading a chapter from the book *Stranger by the River* by Paul Twitchell, modern-day founder of ECKANKAR. In the following quote from page 73 of *The Golden Heart*, Mahanta Transcripts, Book 4, I describe the unique nature of this book.

> Stranger by the River *is actually indicative of what happens between Master and Soul on the inner planes during the initiation. It is the meeting by the river; not the great wave of God, but a river. The Master and the chela sit down together on luxurious grass, and they talk about ECK.*

As you read "The Trembling of a Star," chapter 23 in *Stranger by the River,* imagine you're in that beautiful setting. What do you see and hear? And what are your impressions as you read the poetic words of ECK Master Rebazar Tarzs?

✎

120

This Month's Exercise

A technique to open your heart to greater love
for God and prepare for a future initiation, p. 113

8.   *Before you do your spiritual exercises this
month, I ask you to read chapter 23, "The
Trembling of a Star." It deals with the ECK
initiation in a beautiful and memorable way, a
reminder to each of the Star of God. There you
will learn what the ECK initiation means in
clear and simple terms.* (p. 113)

Your daily spiritual exercise is to sing HU and
contemplate on chapter 23 in *Stranger by the
River* by Paul Twitchell.

Let your mind gently play with the words
and images. Wonder about it as the Mahanta,
the Inner Master, opens your heart to a new
understanding of the ECK initiation. What
insights were revealed to you?

continued

This Month's Exercise *continued*

Extra Writing Page
for this month's exercises and experiences

Peddar Zaskq
(Paul Twitchell)

Sri Harold Klemp,
the Mahanta,
the Living ECK Master

Yaubl Sacabi

Rebazar Tarzs

Kata Daki

Fubbi Quantz

There are hundreds of ECK Masters who work in secret among the human race today. . . .

The ECK Masters serve as models and guides for people who desire truth. (p. 129)

7

The Master Principle

$\asterisk$

ecently, I had a discussion with an ECK writer who plans to write a book about the teachings of ECK. "One aim worthy of achieving," I said, "is to give your reader a true understanding of what a Master is." A puzzled look crossed the writer's face.

This subject of Mastership is important to you because it remains the highest ambition that anyone can have in life.

I went on to explain the false impressions that people carry with them about a spiritual master. First is the idea that a master can change a law, natural or man-made, to serve his own ends. A real Master seldom does that. He tries to let others have room to breathe. Nor will he change the natural order of events, for he knows that everything in life is in its rightful place. Only in a case of urgent need—where the spiritual welfare of a person, a people, or a nation is at stake—will he step in to alter the outcome of a situation.

People have all kinds of odd ideas about a Master. Another is that divine love protects him from hardship or danger. That's the general impression. On the other hand, these people can often recite a list of the many problems or ills that have befallen a certain Master.

They cannot tie the ends together. They don't know how the human and divine qualities of a Master blend, so they divide them into two separate areas. As the centuries pass, people downplay the human side of a Master because it is too ordinary, but they place his divine qualities on a level so high that the average person despairs of ever reaching it.

The outcome in history is an idol made by human hands.

Blending the Human and Divine

How does all this apply to you? The inborn goal of Soul is to become an explorer and a servant of life. Perhaps the meek shall inherit the earth, but only those who are strong in spirit will enter the highest reaches of heaven.

The Mastership principle spoken of here is the one given in the ECK teachings. An ECK Master is a true blend of the human and divine qualities in a human being. He or she is both a person and a principle.

The average person often holds to another fallacy about a real Master: the image of total perfection. The idea is that an ECK Master, or any other master, has reached the peak of unfoldment and no longer cares about new arenas of growth and learning, simply because they do not exist for him. Fortunately, life offers a brighter promise than a snuffed candle, for there is always one more step to go. It is the plus factor in spiritual law.

Many people also believe that an ECK Master can accomplish any goal with little effort, whether it be for health, money, freedom, happiness, or peace of mind.

A Master's Walk

Actually, it is harder for a Master. No matter what his plan or direction, each step is over a path of thorns and sharp rocks. If anything, a Master's walk is more difficult. Even something as routine as getting a pair of contact lenses from a skilled eye doctor demands a major output of time and energy. A doctor's aide places an order with the wrong prescription, and the company that is to make the lenses runs into long delays. Once the wrong lenses come in and the doctor discovers the mistake, the whole procedure starts over for round two.

So one quality of Mastership is patience.

Even those people who are fortunate to be in the inner circle of the Living ECK Master have mistaken ideas about their relationship with him. Often they don't hear or understand him correctly. Yet those are the very ones who rush off to lay decrees or directions upon others in his name, unaware of the damage they do in the spiritual lives of others. The Living ECK Master then has to go back and patch up the injuries.

Thus, who actually does understand the Master?

Some people of narrow mind and perception also feel that a Master has no need for human companionship. Isn't communion with God enough? This attitude belies the fact of human existence and puts on a pedestal the highest ideal that occurs to their all-too-fallible minds: union with God means a separation from human needs. Again, it is the mind-set of idolaters. When these people learn of some human interests of a Master that go against their image of what a real Master should be, it shakes their faith. The problem all along has been their own bondage to a false image about him and the ECK Mastership.

Your Relationship with the Mahanta

I mention these fallacies about Mastership to help you define the main purpose of your relationship with the Mahanta, the Living ECK Master. It is to have his aid in reaching the heights of divine love. You may call this God Consciousness or an experience in the Light and Sound of ECK, but it all adds up to opening your heart to a greater capacity for love.

Love is the simplicity of ECK.

You alone are responsible to SUGMAD (God) for the direction of your life. The Mahanta, the Living ECK Master is the agent of SUGMAD who has the duty to help you become one with the ECK, or Divine Spirit. The Master's life is not yours to own. If he does or says something you do not understand or agree with, it is due to your inability to see truth in a clear light. After all, the purpose of illusion is to blind. You, and you alone, must eventually pierce the cloud of illusion to see the workings of God. The Master is there to help you do so.

Divine Law of Love

Let me say, the average human being has a broken and distorted sense of divine law. He mixes the eternal precepts with his own puny understanding, then tries to impose his imperfect rules upon everyone else as a rigid guide. This bias was behind the Catholic Church's use of the Inquisition in the Middle Ages.

As stated earlier, the Master principle is of two parts: the divine and the human. The ECK Masters embody the divine law of love, and through them it reaches out into all the worlds, creating a wide circle of influence.

A Master says, "I am that I AM." This is a recognition

of his union with Divine Spirit, which exists in all places and time at once. A true Master is in all places at the same time, a pure channel for the limitless power of ECK. He has access to the full knowledge and wisdom of God. The mere fact of having these abilities, of course, is not clear to most people who come in contact with him. Thus, they measure him with a short ruler.

An odd trait of human nature is to weigh everything by human standards. The scale drifts off center and gives a false reading, yet the owner regards it as a machine in good working order. But in the scope of spiritual terms, it is much in need of fixing.

Who Are the ECK Masters?

Who are these people who are the living and breathing embodiment of the Master principle? Will you meet them in ECK? How will they appear? And most of all, what role do they play in your spiritual life?

There are hundreds of ECK Masters who work in secret among the human race today. Most of their names are not in the ECK works, but ECKists meet them in various places—both here and in the higher worlds. A handful of these Masters work directly with those on the path of ECK, working with the Mahanta to guide people to the Temples of Golden Wisdom and other places helpful for their spiritual unfoldment. The ECK Masters are both men and women. Each has gained God Consciousness, and each has gone through the trials of everyday living. What you will find striking about them is their love and compassion, which flows from them like a stream of goodness and light.

The ECK Masters serve as models and guides for people who desire truth.

Meeting the Mahanta

The leader of the spiritual hierarchy is the Mahanta, the Living ECK Master. Chosen by the SUGMAD, he is the chief agent for God, and his first duty is always to show the truth seeker the difference between what is real and what is not. His spiritual name is Wah Z, or often Z for short. He is a seasoned explorer who often travels in the many regions of heaven, like others in the Vairagi Order of ECK Masters.

You will know him by his blue clothing. Wah Z is the inner form of the Outer Master, the individual you know as the Mahanta, the Living ECK Master. At times he appears in glasses.

Peddar Zaskq

Another ECK Master you may meet in your dreams is Peddar Zaskq. That is the spiritual name of Paul Twitchell, who first brought the ECK teachings to the public from 1965 to 1971. Peddar is short in stature. Also dressed in blue much of the time, he has the sturdy upper torso of a boxer, one of his many interests before reaching God Consciousness. Round of face, he has piercing blue eyes. Sometimes they sparkle like diamonds in the sun, and at other times you will have the sensation of looking into the depths of a deep, clear lake.

Peddar often appeared to me in my dreams. Upon awakening, I always had the sense of meeting a friend I had known for ages. Later, I learned that he had been my companion and protector a long time before I first heard the name of ECKANKAR.

Rebazar Tarzs

Next among the ECK Masters you are likely to meet during the dream state or Soul Travel is Rebazar Tarzs.

Like the other ECK Masters, he pays special attention to a certain group of people who used to be chelas (spiritual students) when he served his term as the Mahanta, the Living ECK Master. All who are fortunate to meet this Tibetan ECK Master note his dark, flashing eyes. Rebazar is above average in height. His usual clothing is a knee-length maroon robe with hood. He helps the Mahanta teach ECK members about the love and wisdom of God.

Some people find him too direct for their liking. He surely does not mince words. There is an air of purpose about him, and those who meet him are sure to receive some blessing from it. He came to me often during my years as a spiritual student in ECK. As with Paul, I came to regard Rebazar as a prized and true friend who knew the secret of God. And he was always ready to share it— when I was ready to receive it.

You will recognize Rebazar Tarzs by his dark beard, deep brown eyes, maroon robe, but especially by his direct, no-nonsense manner.

Kata Daki

Kata Daki is a female ECK Master who inspires a desire for God by her benevolence, wisdom, and compassion. Her hair varies in color from honey-blond to a soft brown, and she is taller than average. Like the other ECK Masters, Kata Daki takes a special interest in people who have been close to her in past lives, but she always leads them to the Mahanta as the Wayshower. She may appear in your dreams clothed in a dress, a robe, or a suit. Whatever the fashion she adopts, it is fitting for the time and place. The feeling that people get while in her presence is one of spaciousness and joy, for she is a channel for the Light and Sound of God: divine love in expression.

She and the other ECK Masters each have an area of

special interest. Her pet project is to help people get back on their feet during hardship, helping them to locate food, shelter, and clothing for their families. She is very active during a recession, war, or famine.

Fubbi Quantz

Fubbi Quantz is another ECK Master you are likely to meet in your dream travels. He is in charge of the Katsupari Monastery in Tibet, where he watches over a section of the Shariyat-Ki-Sugmad, the holy book of ECK. He is a tall, elderly man with white hair, a beard, and a gentle smile. Good humor beams from his eyes. Paul Twitchell once described him as having a lantern jaw, and the description fits. Usually Fubbi appears in a long, white robe. Those who can sit in on his classes of the Shariyat are fortunate indeed, for he passes on the Light and Music of God to all who are worthy.

Yaubl Sacabi

Yaubl Sacabi is another ECK Master you should know about. A robust man about the height of Wah Z, he is nevertheless much more sturdy in physical frame. He was the Mahanta, the Living ECK Master among the ancient Greeks, helping to set up the mystery schools. Now his station is the Temple of Golden Wisdom in the spiritual city of Agam Des, located in the Hindu Kush.

Entrance to the city is by invitation only, and then only in the Soul body.

You will recognize Yaubl immediately by his bald head, which gleams like a highly polished golden dome. He has a strong nose, thick neck, and well-developed muscles in his arms and chest. Yet you'll find his main interest is in helping you and others learn the secret laws of life and so make your existence here one of meaning.

There are other spiritual Adepts. Each of them reached the heights of God-Realization in some remote span of history but then went on to yet higher states of awareness. In time, you will meet many of them in your travels.

Let the desire for truth and wisdom be your guide.

This Month's Exercise

The spiritual exercise this month is to help you meet some of the ECK Masters named above.

Let me assure you, if you are a member of ECK, it is because of a close bond between you and one of these spiritual Adepts in the past. You are with an old friend again.

Find a quiet place where you can spend a good twenty minutes without any interruptions. First settle yourself in bed, on a couch, or on the floor. Then calm your mind by softly humming or singing a few minutes of a lullaby you learned as a child.

In the second half of this exercise shut your eyes, if you have not already done so. Now begin to sing *Alayi* (ah-LAH-yee). It is a spiritually charged word you may use to gain access to ECK persons and places here in this world. As you sing *Alayi*, you may choose to put your attention upon one of the ECK Masters described above.

If you stick with this program, you will gain in love, wisdom, and spiritual freedom.

Workbook Activities

1.   *The Mastership principle spoken of here is the one given in the ECK teachings. An ECK Master is a true blend of the human and divine qualities in a human being. He or she is both a person and a principle.* (p. 126)

   Do any of the qualities of—or fallacies about— ECK Mastership surprise you as you read this lesson? What catches your attention? You can underline or highlight these parts in your discourse.

   To meet some of the ECK Masters, try this month's spiritual exercise on page 133.

2.   *This subject of Mastership is important to you because it remains the highest ambition that anyone can have in life.* (p. 125)

   Have you considered that you may be in training for Mastership? Ask the Mahanta, the inner teacher, to show you a quality of Mastership that you are developing right now. You can write your experience here if you wish.

Your Relationship with the Mahanta (p. 128)

3. 🎧 **Audio Excerpt 8**

This excerpt from the talk "Walk with Me, Mahanta" describes the inner and outer role of the Mahanta. After you listen to it, read the following quote from your discourse:

> *I mention these fallacies about Mastership to help you define the main purpose of your relationship with the Mahanta, the Living ECK Master. It is to have his aid in reaching the heights of divine love. You may call this God Consciousness or an experience in the Light and Sound of ECK, but it all adds up to opening your heart to a greater capacity for love.* (p. 128)

Here's an easy way to accept this help being offered you. In the space below, you can make a general request for his aid, or you can ask the Mahanta, the Living ECK Master for spiritual help with a situation in your life.

4.   You may want answers to the questions raised in the quote below.

> *Who are these people who are the living and breathing embodiment of the Master principle? Will you meet them in ECK? How will they appear? And most of all, what role do they play in your spiritual life?* (p. 129)

Several ECK Masters are introduced to you on pages 130–33.

What quality or trait stands out for each Master? You can jot it down here beneath the name of the Master. Perhaps this will help you recognize that Master during your inner travels.

Wah Z
(Sri Harold Klemp,
the Mahanta,
the Living ECK Master)

Peddar Zaskq
(Paul Twitchell)

Rebazar Tarzs

Kata Daki

Fubbi Quantz

Yaubl Sacabi

5.   *The ECK Masters serve as models and guides for people who desire truth.* (p. 129)

Why do you suppose you are being introduced to other ECK Masters? Ask the Mahanta, the Inner Master, to show you what role the ECK Masters play in your spiritual life. You can write about your insights here.

This Month's Exercise

A technique to meet some of the ECK Masters,
p. 133

6.   The spiritual exercise for this month begins in
a unique and enjoyable way:

> *First settle yourself in bed, on a couch, or
> on the floor. Then calm your mind by softly
> humming or singing a few minutes of a
> lullaby you learned as a child.* (p. 133)

What lullaby worked for you? Are there other
ways you've discovered to calm your mind in
preparation for your spiritual exercises? Record
your tips here to try again in the future.

7.   *The spiritual exercise this month is to help
          you meet some of the ECK Masters named
          above.*

          *Let me assure you, if you are a member of
          ECK, it is because of a close bond between you
          and one of these spiritual Adepts in the past.
          You are with an old friend again.* (p. 133)

     Which ECK Master are you drawn to? Who
     would you like to spend a little time with?

     As you do the daily spiritual exercise to meet
     this ECK Master, this old friend, you can
     record your experiences here or in your jour-
     nal. (If you need more space, use page 141.)

     How did you connect with this Master? Did
     you have a dream or daydream? An experi-
     ence in contemplation? An impression,
     knowingness, or memory?

Tip: If you would like to find out more about
     these ECK Masters and others, you can read about
     them in ECK books such as *Those Wonderful ECK
     Masters* and *ECK Masters and You: An Illustrated
     Guide.*

Spotlight on ECK
Noticing and Remembering the Spiritual Gifts

8.   *If you stick with this program, you will gain in love, wisdom, and spiritual freedom.* (p. 133)

Take a moment to look back on this past month. What's one way you've grown spiritually? One thing you've gained to help you on your spiritual quest?

Extra Writing Page
for this month's exercises and experiences

Rebazar Tarzs, the great Tibetan ECK Master, speaks to the seeker, the seeker's mate, and to you: "I will whisper to thee, dear ones, this divine secret.... All things will gravitate to thee if ye will let love enter thine own hearts, without compromise." (p. 151)

8

Can We Live in a World without Love?

✳

*O*urs is a warring universe. It is like a boiling pot on a stove. From ancient times on, people have gone out of their way to rob, injure, maim, or kill each other, often in the name of some deity.

Jeremiah, the "weeping prophet" of the Old Testament, lived around 600 BC, during the exile of the nation of Israel in Babylon. As chief spokesman for his people, he was most acutely aware of the gap between the Lord's promises of peace, for all around him was the clear evidence of a people in slavery.

"Then said I, Ah, Lord God! surely thou hast greatly deceived this people and Jerusalem, saying, Ye shall have peace; whereas the sword reacheth unto the soul" (Jeremiah 4:10).

A promise of peace, but a sword in the heart?

Why the contradiction? The answer, then as ever, lay in the way people trampled the Law of Love in their dealings with others. Perhaps the spiritual trap of all time is the teaching of revenge: an eye for an eye, and a tooth for a tooth.

It, by itself, insures war.

Mostly, the human race has always been milling around in a state of confusion, like an ant lost in the mud. The promises of peace by leaders in politics and religion simply do not bear fruit, for the proofs of strife are more in evidence than ever.

The sketch above is dismal, to be sure. Yet if life had nothing better to offer us—no hope or chance of a better tomorrow—the human race would have run itself into the ground eons ago. In fact, if the future of the human race were up to the selfish and willful appetites of people, this planet would long ago have become a smoldering cinder. People of power love to hate. In that sentence is a main reason for Soul's exile in the lower worlds: to learn love through life's unerring remedy for wrongs.

Who, then, is the real author and editor of world affairs?

Fortunate for us, a power greater than a mere representative of the human race is in final charge of human affairs. This force, at once the hope and mainstay of life, is the ECK. Rising from the heart of God, It flows out into creation like some giant ocean wave—and returns to Its source. The ECK is the Voice of God. In literature, writers have called It the Holy Spirit, the Holy Ghost, the Spirit of Truth, the Spirit of Love, and many other poetic names. In ECKANKAR, we know this Divine Spirit as the Sound and Light of God. They are Its two main aspects.

Path of Love

But for all the words, the Sound and Light of God are simply the expression of love. And so, the path of ECK is the path of love. It is learning how to love yourself, God, and others.

For my part, I came into ECK out of an attraction for

Soul Travel. Others come because of an interest in dreams, healing, a desire to know the future, and many other reasons. And, of course, they find what they are looking for, and a whole lot more. The person with the highest motive of all is the one who comes to ECK in search of love. It took me years to discover that.

In the beginning, I had little or no use for a closer relationship with God. Didn't I already have it? My God was a personal God, a blend between the often angry Lord of the Old Testament who caused fear, and the New Testament's God of love.

A personal God with these extremes of love and anger inside me caused a clash of conflicting emotions: doubt, fear, and worry.

Fear leaves very little room for love.

Every religion has its people of love and power. It is human nature. Each person walks a unique path to God, though a few members in every religion or group are further along the path. These are the saints and holy ones. If one could point to a single quality in which they abound, it would be in the fact of an open, loving heart. These saints, scattered here and there throughout the world, are people who serve others in quiet ways.

Those who love life, serve life.

Frankly, it took me a while to go beyond the merits of Soul Travel and learn about the all-encompassing power of love. My background was Christian, so I loved and read the Bible. During the years of my preministerial study, from high school through college, I took a special delight in the home devotions my mother had our family do several times a week. She was a staunch Christian, but no more than I.

She would select one of my brothers or me to read from a prayer booklet. After that, we read from yet a second book of prayer, so family devotions often lasted ten or fifteen minutes—about the limit for my younger siblings to handle before bedtime.

The longer I went to the religious school, the more smug I became about my piety. One weekend, during my visit home, she had me lead the family devotions. I droned on well beyond the time limit, reading two or three prayers more than usual. Finally, even she—the devoted Christian—had had enough.

"That's all," she said abruptly. And my turn at devotions ended for that evening.

The curt ending was a humbling experience. My brothers jumped from the couch in relief, and one quickly turned on the TV set. But my mother's quick end to my devotions had touched a raw nerve, which left me hurt and confused. Wasn't reading a long devotion a way to show love for God? I began to wonder about the nature of true spirituality.

What Is Spiritual Living?

For me, spiritual living was piety—the devotion and reverence to God and family. The focus of my piety centered upon obeying the will of God, hating myself when I did not live up to the Ten Commandments, and promising God to do it right tomorrow. Life was a whipsaw. No matter what experience came into my life, it was simply another way to suffer spiritual defeat in two ways at once.

You see, piety rests upon outer behavior. This is the reason some religious people, who are models of piety, are often without compassion. Their acts of reverence are merely a response to some mental notion of what others might take to be the sign of a saintly person. Yet their hearts are cold stones, barren of love.

Only the Spirit of Love can break through the crust of

such a heart to let the Light and Sound of God enter.

The mere fact that you found the teachings of ECK in this lifetime is an expression of God's love for you. "Soul exists because God loves It," says *The Shariyat-Ki-Sugmad*, the holy book of ECK. All who come across the ECK teachings do so by invitation of the Mahanta, the Living ECK Master. Good karma has brought this happy occasion to them. Before their birth into this life, the Mahanta met with the Lords of Karma to arrange for the exact setting into which they would come through birth.

Your family, the community, the moment of your birth in the scrolls of history—all play a part in your spiritual growth.

In other ECK writings or talks you'll learn more about the actual ways the Sound and Light of God appear to people. Whatever the way, whether in a dream, a vision, or in daily life, they are a gift far greater than any blessing by a temporal leader. They are a direct gift of God.

So what is the benefit of ECK?

Returning Love to Others

All who have felt the love of God must return that love to others. It is the Law of Love. This law supports the universes, and it is the only hope of peace in your time. That peace never comes through any decree by a leader in politics or religion, for it already resides in the heart, but one must first find it.

Life is hard on purpose. Hardship makes people seek the spirit of imagination and creation within them, for none would do so otherwise. Our imagination, used rightly, is the most godlike part of us.

How do the Sound and Light of God work in the life of the average ECK member? To illustrate, let's look at a woman who works in nutrition. One of her clients had problems sleeping, so she did everything she could to give him a good night's rest through a better diet. Yet nothing helped him. In spite of her methods being unable to bring the patient sleep, he kept pressing her for other avenues of hope.

The nutritionist is an ECKist. Careful to cherish the rights of others, she lets them have their spiritual values and opinions. However, when her client insisted upon another meeting to address his sleep problem, she agreed.

Before the consultation, she asked the Mahanta to give her the words to speak. When the client arrived, she mainly listened. In the back of her mind, however, was the principle of goal setting, learned from an ECK teacher in a Satsang class.

So, using her imagination, she used that principle in the context of her patient's problem with sleep.

"What is your exact goal?" she asked him. Could he explain what a perfect night's sleep would be like? How would it differ from what he was having now?

He told of his terror, how he stalled as long as possible to keep from having to lie down in bed and face sleep. The Mahanta nudged her to ask what other times he had felt this numbing fear. He told of several alarming events in his life, but she felt that none of them was the real source of the fear. She urged him back to his childhood, when he was a little boy. Did he have any trouble sleeping as a child? He began to shake noticeably.

How did his mother deal with his sleep problems?

By now, her patient sat rigid and trembling in his chair. "Every night," he said, "this is how I feel. Only now it's worse."

The ECK inwardly urged her to get more details, though

she was sailing in uncharted waters. Another scene came to mind as he recalled how his desperate mother had repeatedly tried to force him to sleep by covering his head with a blanket. It was the cause of his terror. He began to cry when he realized that his fear of sleep was due to this memory of his mother. As a child, he thought she was trying to kill him.

He looked at the nutritionist in wonder. Now sixty, he'd spent a fortune over the years to try to cure his problem, but nobody else had even come close to uncovering the pain that had dogged him so long.

She tried to tell him about the perfect timing of Divine Spirit. However, he didn't care to know more than the reason for his fear, so she saved the greater knowledge about ECK for another time. She feels grateful for the gift of being an instrument of Spirit for even a few moments: a state of grace that defies words. Her practice in nutrition opens the door to many other golden opportunities.

Yet she wonders how much she can tell people about the insights that the ECK gives her. She asked, "In a counseling situation, is it within the spiritual laws to reveal some of these things?"

It pays to use good judgment. Since most people can only handle so much truth at once, it's simply wiser to give help as an instrument for Divine Spirit and let people put forward any questions about ECK on their own. It's like the old story about a young child who says to his mother, "Tell me about my birth." So the mother takes a deep breath to take on the delicate task of sex education. When she finishes her lecture about the origin of babies, the child says, "I just want to know if I was born in Brooklyn."

The nutritionist has a heart of love. Because of that, the ECK has a clear way to reach out and improve the lot of many people who come to her for aid.

Once a woman came to her with much pain in her eyes. The nutritionist saw that the woman was afraid to live and even more terrified to die. "What should I do?" the woman pleaded. The nutritionist said, "You have to find your spiritual path, whatever that is." Although her client thanked her for the answer, it was clear she wanted more information. This left the nutritionist in a quandary. How much should she tell this woman about ECK? Instead of giving her client a lot of words, she tried instead to give her love.

No one ever goes wrong by giving divine love to those in need.

Two Approaches to Life

There are two approaches to life as there are indeed to ECK: the way of the heart versus that of the mind. In the first class are all who heed the gentle whisperings of Spirit and move in harmony with life around them. They are giants on the path of love. The other, far larger group is of those who deal with problems largely with the mind and are usually pawns of their fickle emotions. So they set their will above divine guidance. They simply do not know how to accept Spirit's lead. These people try to force people and events to go against the natural order of Divine Spirit, through the misuse of laws, logic, and other means of control.

In the end, the raw experiences of life purge each of us. Pain and hardship create a clean heart. The pot of life boils hot, but that's how the impurities of the human state leave us.

You are Soul. You are a divine creation of God. You have unlimited powers of imagination at your disposal to create a new and better place for yourself in life. You alone must do it. Even the Mahanta lets you walk your own path to God, offering help and advice only if you open the petals of your heart. That is the purpose of the Spiritual Exercises of ECK.

They are your key to love, wisdom, and understanding. One follows below.

This Month's Exercise

The spiritual exercise for this month zeroes in on divine love. Each day, if possible, take the following quote from *Stranger by the River* into contemplation for twenty minutes. Shut your eyes and think about it gently.

Rebazar Tarzs, the great Tibetan ECK Master, speaks to the seeker, the seeker's mate, and to you: "I will whisper to thee, dear ones, this divine secret. Let thine ears become filled with wisdom and thy hearts with understanding. Now it is this: All things will gravitate to thee if ye will let love enter thine own hearts, without compromise."

There is more to this quote that will help you spiritually. If you wish to read the rest of it, look in chapter 15, "The Loving Heart."

Workbook Activities

1.   *You are Soul. You are a divine creation of God. You have unlimited powers of imagination at your disposal to create a new and better place for yourself in life.* (p. 150)

Can we live in a world without love? What answers and insights light up for you as you read this lesson?

 Want a simple way to focus on divine love? Try this month's spiritual exercise on page 151. It's to contemplate on a passage from *Stranger by the River* by Paul Twitchell.

Path of Love (pp. 144–46)

2.   *The Sound and Light of God are simply the
expression of love. And so, the path of ECK is the
path of love. It is learning how to love yourself,
God, and others.* (p. 144)

🎧 **Audio Excerpt 9**

You can hear more about the purpose of love in
this excerpt from the talk "The Secret of Love."

Then ask the Mahanta, the Inner Master, to show
you one thing you've learned in the past month
about loving yourself, God, or others. What did
you discover?

✎

3.   Contemplate on the following quote for a moment.

> *For my part, I came into ECK out of an attraction for Soul Travel. Others come because of an interest in dreams, healing, a desire to know the future, and many other reasons. . . . The person with the highest motive of all is the one who comes to ECK in search of love.* (pp. 144–45)

What about you? Why are you studying these discourses? Just for fun, in the space below write a short notice, like one you would find in the Help Wanted section of a newspaper. In a few words, describe what you want from a spiritual path.

WANTED:

What Is Spiritual Living? (pp. 146–47)

4. As you read the quote below, you can highlight
    or underline some of the ways the Sound and
    Light—these gifts from God—have appeared to
    you.

> *In other ECK writings or talks you'll learn
> more about the actual ways the Sound and Light of
> God appear to people. Whatever the way, whether
> in a dream, a vision, or in daily life, they are a gift
> far greater than any blessing by a temporal leader.
> They are a direct gift of God.* (p. 147)

Take a few moments to relax and imagine the
Light and Sound of God, the ECK, entering into
your heart. What color is the Light? Do you hear
or feel the Sound? What else do you notice? You
can jot down your experience below.

Returning Love to Others (pp. 147–50)

5. Open your heart to a new look at life's challenges. Ask the Mahanta, the Inner Master, to give you insight into a hardship in your life today. Then read the following quote:

> *Life is hard on purpose. Hardship makes people seek the spirit of imagination and creation within them, for none would do so otherwise. Our imagination, used rightly, is the most godlike part of us.* (p. 147)

As you read the story about the nutritionist on pages 147–50, you can put a star by the keys that may apply to your own challenge.

Two Approaches to Life (pp. 150–51)

6.   *There are two approaches to life as there are indeed to ECK: the way of the heart versus that of the mind.* (p. 150)

You can explore the way of the heart a little more. Write down the name of a person of the heart— someone you know who is open and loving. What's different about this person? How does this person serve life?

7.   *In the first class are all who heed the gentle whisperings of Spirit and move in harmony with life around them. They are giants on the path of love.*
(p. 150)

The next time you feel like you're in a warring universe, try listening for the gentle whisperings of Spirit. What do you hear, or what nudge comes to you? What happens next? You can record your experiences below.

This Month's Exercise

A technique to zero in on divine love, p. 151

8.   *The spiritual exercise for this month zeroes in on divine love. Each day, if possible, take the following quote from* Stranger by the River *into contemplation for twenty minutes. Shut your eyes and think about it gently.*

   . . . "All things will gravitate to thee if ye will let love enter thine own hearts, without compromise." (p. 151)

Each day, treat yourself to the spiritual exercise on page 151. Then take a moment to jot down whatever you experience, even if it's subtle or fleeting.

This journal of perceptions and insights can serve as a reminder of your growing connection with the ECK, Divine Spirit.

Extra Writing Page
for this month's exercises and experiences

To reach these places during your periods of contemplation, first chant the name of the ECK Temple that has caught your fancy, then *Alayi* (ah-LAH-yee). (p. 165)

9

The God Worlds— Where No One Has Gone Before?

*W*olfgang A. Mozart said, "Neither a lofty degree of intelligence nor imagination nor both together go to the making of genius. Love, love, love, that is the soul of genius."

It is precisely love that makes possible any venture into the unseen regions of God, the heavens that are the stuff of the afterlife for most religions. In ECK, our desire is to see the heavens now, in this lifetime. We want to have a goal like a crew member on *Star Trek*'s starship *Enterprise*: "To boldly go where no man has gone before."

In fact, however, people do travel to the regions of God in this lifetime, but they simply don't remember. The purpose of the teachings of ECK is to help them, and you, remember.

The *Star Trek* TV show proclaims, "Space—the final frontier!" This is not exactly so. The frontiers of earth have fallen, one by one, to the curiosity of its foremost inhabitants—at least we people like to think of ourselves as such. Is space travel the final frontier? While it presents a major step forward in the annals of human history, the spiritual records have long told of adventurers who risked the unknown and went into the invisible worlds. They used natural means.

With no clumsy or wasteful propulsion motors, like our fire-breathing rockets, to hinder them, they instead relied upon the force of their inner powers. Yet a traveler needs a map to show the way in a foreign area, or the aid of someone who knows the territory.

A Guide in Foreign Territory

The guide in ECKANKAR is the Mahanta, the Living ECK Master. He is always on the move in the invisible worlds, going here and there to bring comfort and relief to the lonely and weary. As a servant of life, he helps all sorts of people, situations, and environments. His experience is your gain. He has both the means and the spiritual power to help you travel into the higher worlds of God. He has the map. Of a truth, he is a welcome travel companion, someone who can give you advice and help at any crossing on the path home to God.

So in this discourse, let's review your travel route to the other worlds. You need to know a few key rules and facts before you get too far along on your inner journey, for a little knowledge now spares you from needless worry later.

Keep one important point in mind before we start. While knowledge about what to do and where to go in the invisible worlds of God is useful data, the power of love will get you through any difficulty. Love simplifies the journey to God. The information here is useful, but the secret of knowing how to open your heart to divine love is priceless. How to attain the latter is the purpose of the Spiritual Exercises of ECK. Many of the areas listed below have a word to chant in a certain way, which will help to open your heart to the loving mercies of SUGMAD (God) ITSELF.

Some information that follows may seem too simple to bother with. Yet a teacher must repeat, repeat, repeat. People who fail in their endeavors often do so because they neglect the basics; they have a feeling of superiority that works against their spiritual good.

The Physical Plane

The physical universe is the first step on the road to the secret kingdom. It includes your need for a human body, the fact of day-to-day problems, and the challenge of dealing with the forces of illusion.

Pinda is the Sanskrit name for the physical universe. The classical name for it, however, is Elam. The ruler is Elohim, or Elam, a minor god at the foot of the spiritual ladder whose duty is to help with the administration of this universe. His job is to carry out the directives that come from above, to serve people. His helpers include angels and devas, a group of spiritual workers who help people develop the higher emotions and finer intelligence. Angels serve mostly in the role of messengers.

The subjective side of the physical plane is about Soul's effort to deal with the senses. Hearing, sight, smell, touch, and taste provide one with the experiences of pleasure and pain. The senses play upon the body, heart, and mind.

The main Temple of Golden Wisdom on the physical plane is now at Chanhassen, Minnesota. The Seat of Power, it is the destination of ECK chelas who go there nightly with the Mahanta in their Soul bodies to learn the divine knowledge of the Shariyat-Ki-Sugmad. The section of the Shariyat taught there gives a foretaste of the secret works of ECK, and the guardian is the spiritual leader of ECKANKAR.

Five Golden Wisdom Temples

A total of five Temples of Golden Wisdom exist on the physical plane. Next is the Faqiti Monastery, hidden in the Gobi Desert and a way station for nightly travelers who come there in the Soul form to learn about the wisdom of ECK. The ECK Master in charge there is a mysterious person by the name of Banjani. He gives an introduction to the spiritual works of ECK to all who are so fortunate as to find their way to this remote part of the world. ECKists come here by dream or Soul travel only.

Third of the Golden Wisdom Temples is the Katsupari Monastery in northern Tibet. Here, Fubbi Quantz is guardian of the first section of the Shariyat, "The Chronicles of ECK." Here also are the Kadath Inscriptions, which give a history of all Living ECK Masters from the earliest times. Besides these records, one also may view the Naacal records, which give a look at human civilization from the very beginning. This monastery is near the Valley of Shangta, site of the passing of the Rod of ECK Power, when the Living ECK Master turns the leadership of ECK over to his successor. The Oracle of Tirmer is also nearby.

Fourth among the Golden Wisdom Temples is Gare-Hira, the Temple of Golden Wisdom at Agam Des ("inaccessible place"), one of several spiritual cities around the globe. The Adepts here carry the striking name of God-eaters, because they devour the cosmic energies for sustenance instead of ordinary food. Agam Des is also a way station for interplanetary spacecraft.

The guardian at Gare-Hira is the renowned ECK Master Yaubl Sacabi. One comes by invitation only. The essence of his teaching is that the destiny of each person is to become a Co-worker with God, which brings spiritual freedom, wisdom, and charity.

Last among the nearby Temples of Golden Wisdom is the House of Moksha in Retz, the capital city of Venus. The ECK guardian at this "house of liberation" is Rami Nuri, who teaches the gospel of salvation in this lifetime from the rounds of births and deaths. He points the way to the ECKshar, a state of high consciousness on the Soul level. One who reaches the ECKshar can know the past, present, and future for himself and others if he is willing to undergo the direct, strict discipline needed to learn the ECK-Vidya, the ancient science of prophecy.

A striking feature of the House of Moksha is a translucent dome at one end of the large temple complex. Of course, this site is a supraphysical one, existing above the normal range of human vision. Yet our space explorers may someday detect its location by the unusual vibrations in the area.

Thus, the Mahanta takes new members of ECK to each of these Golden Wisdom Temples in the order stated above.

To reach these places during your periods of contemplation, first chant the name of the ECK Temple that has caught your fancy, then *Alayi* (ah-LAH-yee). It's the word to use when trying to reach a location on the physical plane. For example, softly sing *Moksha-alayi* for ten or fifteen minutes during your spiritual exercise to meet Rami Nuri. For most people, this will take several or more tries. For the Temple of ECK in Chanhassen, chant *ECK-alayi*.

If successful, you may expect to hear the sound of thunder and see either a white, blue, or green light in your inner vision.

The Astral Plane

The Astral is the next plane of the God Worlds beyond the Physical. It marks the limits of astral projection, a risky method of travel in inner space because the teachers of the astral system of exploration are, in a manner of speaking, novices at the game. The worlds of the Astral Plane rank as the lowest of the heavens. Yet it is the location of the Astral powerhouse, which sustains life in the whole physical universe below. This plane is also home to the native religions, such as animism.

The classical name for the Astral Plane is Turiya (also, Tirkya) Pad. Egg-shaped, it also carries the name of Anda (egg). This place is a blend of matter and spirit, but with a greater ratio of spirit in the mix than on the Physical Plane. Thus, we can say that its atomic structure is lighter and finer than that of the physical.

The Astral Plane has a variety of heavens, hells, and purgatories (or more accurately, reformatories). People rest here until it is time to return to another human body and continue working off the lessons of old and new karma.

The ruler here is a lesser god: Jot Niranjan, sometimes known as Sat Kanwal—the Jehovah of the Old Testament. You may meet him sometime in your travels with the Mahanta, but for all his bluster, Jot Niranjan can only treat you like a guest instead of an inmate within his keep. The protection of the Mahanta is one of the benefits you gain on the path of ECK. You will find the Astral region to be a place of interest, for it is the source of many flying saucers, ghosts, and the seat of emotions.

In this world, your outer covering is a starry body. It is the link between your mind and physical self, which must struggle with the five senses and the emotions of pain and pleasure.

How Emotions Influence You

The Astral Plane governs most of human action. From it spring such emotions as anger, in which frustration leads to feelings of hostility toward oneself, his situation, or his environment. An example may be a teen who chafes under the rules of his parents. Soul, like that young person, must learn a healthy outlet for hostility of that sort, or suffer the likes of a lost friendship or career. The willful destruction of private or public property and fits of bad temper are signs of aggression that spring from the emotion of anger. So are rage and hate.

Another emotion that Soul must learn to control while in the human playground is anxiety. A fear caused by a real or imagined threat, it cuts one off from the love and esteem of nearby people. It constricts the heart. Signs of it are tension, headache, a tired feeling, and scores of aches and pains. Emotions are a trap for those who look in vain for the Mahanta, for only he can loosen the grip of the emotions so love can enter in.

The emotion of fear has the uncanny ability to make one freeze into a cake of ice. Fear is partly a behavior learned after birth, but pain quickly adds to the burden of karma that the individual has brought with him or her from the past, until it becomes hard for such people to act at all.

When a person fears something, he first goes into a state of heightened awareness. Then the adrenaline begins to flow. His activity slows as he puts full attention upon the source of danger, making him move more slowly and carefully. Next, fear causes him to lose control of his emotions as he begins to sweat and his breathing becomes shallow. His heart rate climbs. In war or in other crises, like a building fire, people have lost control—shouting or laughing or crying—then run right into the worst danger.

167

The price of losing control of their emotions was the final sacrifice—losing their own life.

Learning to Deal with Emotions

Usually, we think of our emotions in terms of how we feel about something. Our experiences range from agreeable to unpleasant feelings, from excitement to depression.

Envy and jealousy are two extreme emotions. Envy, the lesser of the two, is having a desire for something that others have, like the fruit of their work or effort: a good home, many possessions, a happy family, or even something as hard to steal as a joyful or peaceful heart. As destructive as envy is, it only eats upon the peace of mind of the individual so infected.

Jealousy is worse. We can sum up jealousy as those sour feelings toward another whom we view as having taken those privileges or rights that belong to us. The main difference between the emotions of envy and jealousy is that jealousy always has the element of hostility in it. Not only does a person fear losing what he has to another, especially in the area of love or affection, but hostility often leads to action that destroys both oneself and others.

An example is that of a jealous suitor and the result that follows his rage. Another example is the unhappy feelings of a child when he feels his parents' love has shifted to a younger brother or sister.

Of course, there are also pleasant emotions, like the delight of a baby. And what is more satisfying than being in love? We also put a large price tag on comfort and relaxation, which make life worth living. A person on top of his emotions usually wears a smile as gladdening as the rays of sunshine at dawn. We treasure such people, or at least we should.

Thus, a person (Soul in the human form) must learn to deal with the emotions. These emotions from the Astral Plane come right into the physical world, having more influence upon the decisions of people and nations than we might think. The human race is now at the second, or Astral, level of spiritual unfoldment. It is no surprise to a student of ECK that people so often act with blind emotions, rather than with a cool head of reason.

This Month's Exercise

The spiritual exercise for this month is to help you move ahead spiritually by learning to cope with your emotions.

The word to use in contemplation is *Kala*, the special word for the Astral Plane. Breathe deeply and chant it four times, then sit in silence for an equal amount of time. Repeat the cycle for ten to fifteen minutes.

This exercise is important. More than one initiate who has been in ECK for some years still has trouble with the play of emotions. The Master will bring your problem areas to light so you may see them clearly. The ECK will then help you lessen their hold upon you through Its power and love.

Love is the genius of ECK.

Workbook Activities

1.   *In ECK, our desire is to see the heavens now, in this lifetime.* (p. 161)

Take a tour of the Physical and Astral planes with a master guide. As you come across parts of this lesson that light up for you, highlight or underline them.

What's one thing that surprises you or stands out for you?

 You can move ahead spiritually by learning to cope with your emotions. This month's spiritual exercise on page 169 shows you how.

2. 🎧 **Audio Excerpt 10**

To hear a description of some Temples of Golden Wisdom in the inner worlds, you can listen to this excerpt from the talk "God Is Speaking through You."

Then read the following:

> *It is precisely love that makes possible any venture into the unseen regions of God....*
> *... Love simplifies the journey to God. The information here is useful, but the secret of knowing how to open your heart to divine love is priceless.* (pp. 161, 162–63)

Do you wonder about the importance of divine love? Ask the Mahanta, the Inner Master, how love can make your journey to God easier.

Open yourself to his response. What do you perceive?

A Guide in Foreign Territory (pp. 162–63)

3.   What parts of the following quote speak directly to you? You can underline or highlight those parts.

✏

> *The guide in ECKANKAR is the Mahanta, the Living ECK Master. He is always on the move in the invisible worlds, going here and there to bring comfort and relief to the lonely and weary. As a servant of life, he helps all sorts of people, situations, and environments. His experience is your gain. He has both the means and the spiritual power to help you travel into the higher worlds of God. He has the map. Of a truth, he is a welcome travel companion, someone who can give you advice and help at any crossing on the path home to God.* (p. 162)

If you wish, you can invite the Mahanta, the Living ECK Master to be your travel companion and guide you into the higher worlds of God.

Five Golden Wisdom Temples (pp. 164–65)

4. Imagine that you're planning a spiritual sight-seeing tour of the Temples of Golden Wisdom. What catches your interest or curiosity as you read the descriptions on pages 164–65?

    Beneath the name of each Temple, jot down something you would like to experience. For example, would you like to meet an ECK Master such as the mysterious Banjani? Or explore the Naacal records, which give a look at human civilization from the very beginning?

Temple of ECK, Chanhassen

Faqiti Monastery, Gobi Desert

Katsupari Monastery, Tibet

Gare-Hira, Agam Des

House of Moksha, Retz

5.   Ready to remember one of your many visits to these Temples of Golden Wisdom? Write down the name of a Temple you would like to visit.

✎

Now try the spiritual exercise given below.

> *Thus, the Mahanta takes new members of ECK to each of these Golden Wisdom Temples....*
>
> *To reach these places during your periods of contemplation, first chant the name of the ECK Temple that has caught your fancy, then* Alayi *(ah-LAH-yee)*. (p. 165)

What did you perceive? Do you feel different? You can jot down any impressions, no matter how subtle. They may come as insights, sensations, feelings, sounds, or colors.

✎

Learning to Deal with Emotions (pp. 168–69)

6.   *Thus, a person (Soul in the human form) must learn to deal with the emotions. These emotions from the Astral Plane come right into the physical world, having more influence upon the decisions of people and nations than we might think.* (p. 169)

Ask the Mahanta, the Inner Master, to show you an example of the influence of emotions. Watch for the play of emotions on TV, in a book or movie, or in others. What do you notice?

7. Experiment with this exercise. First read the following quote:

    A person on top of his emotions usually wears a smile as gladdening as the rays of sunshine at dawn. We treasure such people, or at least we should. (pp. 168–69)

    Then for a few moments, imagine you're on top of your emotions and that your heart is smiling. How does it feel?

This Month's Exercise

A technique to move ahead spiritually by learning to cope with emotions, p. 169

8. *The spiritual exercise for this month is to help you move ahead spiritually by learning to cope with your emotions. . . .*

    . . . The Master will bring your problem areas to light so you may see them clearly. The ECK will then help you lessen their hold upon you through Its power and love. (p. 169)

Would you like to open yourself to more divine love and spiritual freedom? Try the spiritual exercise on page 169 during the month.

Then watch for ways the ECK is helping you lessen the hold of a problem area. Be open to how this help may come: perhaps through a nudge, a dream, an understanding, or a feeling of lightness. The Mahanta, the inner teacher, may suggest a technique to try. Or something you read or hear may light up for you.

You can record your experiences here or in your journal. You can also use the extra writing page (p. 179).

continued

This Month's Exercise *continued*

You may want to mark this exercise on page 169 with a paper clip or bookmark so you can find it easily. It may come in handy in the future, anytime you'd like some help with the play of emotions.

Extra Writing Page
for this month's exercises and experiences

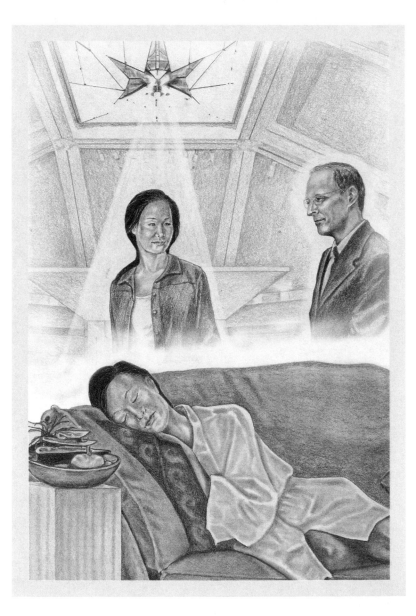

Ask the Mahanta about a health condition, a relationship, or a numbing fear. Then let him guide your dreams,
knowing that love heals all. (p. 190)

10

Ask the Reason, Say BeCAUSE

✦

*I*n this discourse we will look briefly at the planes of cause, thought, and pure Spirit. These, in ECK, are the Causal, Mental (and sometimes Etheric), Soul, and higher planes—in which the Sound and Light of God increase as we rise from the initial to higher levels of awareness. But most of our attention will be on the Causal Plane.

Anyone who has ever listened to a small child knows the pressures on the Answer Man or Answer Mom. Every other sentence begins with "Why?"

"Why don't roly-polies (short, fat bugs) have wings and fly?" Answer: Because then they'd be flies and there are too many already.

"Why do snails eat leaves?" (Snails in our garden ate big holes in the radish and lettuce leaves.) Answer: "Because they're too slow to catch meat for dinner."

"Why do grown-ups tell kids what to do all the time?" Answer: "Because it is one of their few pleasures."

As you can see, a child with questions from morning

till night can strain the resources of a parent, and the answers eventually turn to gibberish. Yet to satisfy the child's questions, the answers must open with *because*. That single word has brought relief to many a harried parent, who can only hope that time will forgive such a doubtful use of a fertile mind in the pursuit of a moment's peace.

Now let's continue with our survey of planes, or heavens, begun in last month's discourse. Each of these planes corresponds to some part of our spiritual makeup.

The Causal Plane

This plane is the source of *because*. The word comes from an old Middle English phrase "bi cause" or "by cause that." It showed the reason for something happening or being. We find this definition for *cause* in the dictionary: "a reason for an action or condition; something that brings about an effect or a result."

It is not by accident that we treat the Causal, Mental, and Etheric Planes together, because they are all of the same group: the broad Mental Plane. The Causal Plane and Causal mind are part of the lower mind. Located right above the Astral Plane, the Causal is the storehouse of karma and memories. It is the source of karmic patterns that cause some people so much grief, but also bring joy to many others.

The Causal body is similar to the Astral body in appearance, but much finer in vibration and more beautiful. Within it are the impressions of all previous lives. Also of interest is that the seed for every condition of your present life was in place already on the Causal Plane before your birth.

In TV mystery shows, the sleuth looks for three elements before he or she can solve a mystery: motive, means, and opportunity. The detective, in making an analysis of the crime, knows that whoever did it had to have a strong reason to take the risk. So what was the motive? Once that piece of the puzzle is on the table, then how did the criminal carry out the crime? What means did the person use? Finally, after our TV detective dusts off more clues, which suspect had the best chance to commit the crime? Once the detective finds the answers to these three questions, the guilty party is off to jail.

In fact, karma and reincarnation are much like a mystery story, because many of the events in a person's life weave around motive, means, and opportunity.

The Causal Plane is a good place to visit during the dream state. The Mahanta, the Living ECK Master often takes the members of ECKANKAR there to give them an idea of what made them what they are today. It is a place of honesty. He shows them the exact reasons for their life situations today, but the dreamer must be open for this inner experience. Many people say they want to know why certain things exist in their life, but in truth they don't actually want to know. That is especially true when the finger of responsibility might point at them. That is one reason initiates grow slack with the Spiritual Exercises of ECK. They want to unfold spiritually, but not if the yoke of blame somehow should fall on them.

Yet that's what makes this world spin around. Earth is a divine classroom, where the pupils all have suitcases full of experiences when they misused the properties of motive, means, and opportunity. They repeatedly gave in to the five passions of lust, anger, greed, vanity, and undue attachment to material goods. Each person has made all his or her own problems.

That is the bitter truth about karma and reincarnation.

Self-Starter or Victim?

People mainly regard the causes of events in one of two ways. One group says that a person is largely the cause of events in life, while the second group feels that forces beyond the control of an individual are the prime movers. Of course, these two philosophies are at odds. Most people, though, fall somewhere between the two extremes, for they feel in control of certain events, but not of others.

Group-one people, the self-starters, are those who believe their thoughts and actions count in getting what life finally offers them. They usually are happy and self-directed people.

Group-two people, the victims, like the role of life's casualties. They think and act as if fate, God's will, and the world is beyond the control of people. Thus, they are often unhappy and usually lack a desire to make anything of life.

So a question that often rises in the minds of some ECK members is, Can an ECKist go to a psychiatrist? Taking it a step further, others might ask, "Then what about a specialist in past-life regression?" In short, most people don't need a psychiatrist any more than they need the casual services of a brain surgeon. Of course, there is a time and place for everything. In an emergency, of course, a person should find a doctor who offers him the best chance of restoring a normal and productive life.

Let's look at an example: a person with an abscessed tooth. Would he get more relief from a dentist or the clergy, from a filling (maybe a root canal) or a prayer? We have to use common sense.

Yet, you argue, deep emotional scars are more serious than a toothache. If it's natural to visit a dentist for a sore tooth, wouldn't it make as much sense to have a psychiatrist treat an injury of the emotions? In some cases, yes. Here again, it's a matter of judgment. It's what sets preventive care in health apart from emergency treatment. A person who is unable to handle the stress of everyday living might well seek a specialist in the medical field, especially when that person has trouble getting along in society. It's a case for emergency help.

A Long-Term Cure

However, most initiates in ECKANKAR are in balance and can go for the long-term cure that comes with the Spiritual Exercises of ECK.

I'll say here that the cures of psychiatry are for the short haul: a few months, years, or maybe even for a lifetime. But is the latter a cure or a sugar pill? Does psychiatry use Band-Aids when a patient actually needs an entire inner cleansing? Can psychiatry go deep enough? Many people in today's consume-it-now society always settle for the quick cure, because they simply don't know the difference. When the same karmic problem comes to the surface again later, they fail to recognize it as the original one.

A superb book on regression therapy is *Through Time into Healing* by Dr. Brian L. Weiss. He works with the basics of the deeper teachings of ECK, and his research adds to the growing body of knowledge about the Astral and Causal Planes. It is not a definitive study by any means. Spiritually, the study is off balance, because it cannot identify and foil the censor, the agent of the mind that does everything in its power to keep us free of emotional pain.

Mind makes a bridge between Soul, our true identity,

and the emotions. The Causal mind remembers past lives, the pure Mental mind empowers, or awakens, the memories in storage, while the Etheric mind has an intuitive feel for what the past means today. When a person has a hunch about something, it is a recall of a similar set of circumstances from the past—and the outcome. It shows the higher mind (the Etheric), the middle (Mental), and the lower (Causal) mind working in accord with each other. They select and feed information to the human emotions.

Dr. Weiss gives many case histories of patients he regressed with hypnosis to help them in their uphill battle to fit better into society. Sometimes his method of treatment takes a patient to the Causal Plane. There, the individual looks at a series of past lives, which an inner guide helps to explain. Yet a faulty seam exists in this chain of analysis, but we will speak of that later.

We'll look at a few of his patients. Notice that each person had a hard time dealing with some problem, and that each past life shed light on its cause.

For years, Elaine, a psychologist, had extreme pains in her neck, shoulders, and upper back. Dr. Weiss also learned during the initial interview that she had a terror of heights and drowning. During her regression therapy, she saw herself standing atop a stone tower, hands tied behind her, and a blindfold in place over her eyes. Everything was black. A soldier in her early twenties, she was on the losing side in a battle. Then an enemy soldier behind her thrust his lance into her back, causing her to fall into the moat where she drowned. After viewing this past life, Elaine lost her fear of heights and drowning. Her back pains also disappeared.

In another life, Elaine was a hopeless male in medieval France who wore filthy clothes and lacked the courage to speak out and take charge of his life. She left that life by the hangman's noose. The authorities sent her to the gallows for a crime she didn't commit.

Right after viewing this experience, her neck pains vanished. Elaine saw how her reluctance to speak out and take charge had followed her into the present from that past life in medieval France. With her health in better shape, she decided to tell the newspapers and others her story.

This time, Dr. Weiss wryly notes, the public gave her their congratulations rather than a hanging.

A second case involved Carole, the wife of Dr. Weiss. Every month for years, the pain and nausea of chronic headaches had disabled her until she finally went to a therapist for help. (She and her husband were too close for him to stay objective with the therapy.) The headaches became even worse after an auto accident, which injured her neck, creating pain for some overhead movements like serving a ball on a tennis court. In a session, the therapist had her ask herself the cause of these migraine headaches.

On the screen of her mind, Carole saw herself, a poor male in filthy burlap clothes, running in front of a mob somewhere in Europe about a thousand years ago. They wanted to punish her for heretical beliefs. When the mob caught her, a severe blow from a club struck her above the left eye, the spot where her migraine was worst. She died from the assault.

But her therapist said, "You no longer need this pain; let it go." And that fast, it disappeared. Nor has a migraine of that severity ever troubled her again.

Very often, trauma from a past life is the source for pain in this incarnation. Alberto, a physician, had for many years suffered from pain and spasms in his back. Two past lives revealed the cause. In one, as a soldier on a battlefield in Europe a few centuries ago, he received a fatal wound to the small of his back.

After therapy, his back pain and muscle spasms soon improved.

A final case to mention from the research of Dr. Weiss is that of Betty, who found regression therapy the means to end her dependence on medicines. From childhood on, she had suffered from asthma, allergies, and other respiratory ailments. She took steroids and shots of adrenaline to help her breathe. In therapy she began to choke, struggling for air. She told Dr. Weiss of a past lifetime in the Middle Ages, where she was burned at the stake. Smoke cut off her oxygen, while heat seared her lungs. Finally, Betty left her body and floated above the crowd, watching the flames destroy her body.

Her asthma got better soon after this session.

This case, and many similar ones, led Weiss to conclude that trauma from the past leaves its residue in the present.

And so it does.

Healing the Past

Yet for all the help that regressive therapy can give to patients in serious need of treatment, there are many others who try this therapy for a lark. They are simply curious about the past. Instead of using self-discipline to travel inside themselves with the Spiritual Exercises of ECK and asking the Mahanta to help them uncover the past, they prefer a lazy route. After all, with a doctor it just takes money. They only want to lay their money down and let the doctor do the work. Yet what do they get in return?

A therapist who uses hypnosis to get at past lives can do some good, of course. There are many cases where people do lead happier lives after therapy. I have no problem with the social or emotional mending that takes place.

However, someone who calls himself a seeker and is not in urgent need of therapy—to fit responsibly into society—is like a newcomer at a horse auction. He puts down his money for a good riding mount but ends up with a wild mustang. Why? Because they look the same to him. His folly could cost a few broken bones down the road, but, after all, isn't that what experience is all about? He'll know better next time.

The fallacy behind hypnotic regression, even by a trained therapist, is that the doctor strays into places in the other worlds that are outside his area of scientific training. For example, the mind censor often allows a patient to have experiences from the past that show how others have wronged him or her. The mind censor wants to protect the individual and so lets such experiences through. It will try all within its power to block out anything that points the finger of cause at the patient. It shields the ego.

Such patients may come from therapy in better shape than in the beginning. Yet their improvement is an illusion. They usually believe that *others* are the cause of their trouble in the past. Of course, there are lessons to learn from that, too, but those are not in line with the precepts of ECK: acceptance of our total responsibility for every act, condition, or state of mind.

How can a therapist tell when a patient's censor has blocked out critical information from the past? He hasn't the spiritual tools to determine that. Only the Mahanta has the spiritual insight and experience to bring about changes that last.

Therapy can put a Band-Aid on a problem and help a patient get by in society. Yet spiritual healing goes far beyond the Causal level—where even most good doctors stop—and takes a person in search of truth to the Soul

Plane and beyond. That is one of the main benefits of ECK. It can heal all your bodies: the human, the emotional, the causal, and the mental. In the end, you become a spiritual being of love and compassion, with true peace, joy, and contentment.

You become a cause of life.

This Month's Exercise

Briefly, the spiritual exercise this month is to chant *Mana* (chanted as mah-NAY). Before you begin it, ask the Mahanta about a health condition, a relationship, or a numbing fear. Then let him guide your dreams, knowing that love heals all.

Workbook Activities

1.   *In this discourse we will look briefly at the planes of cause, thought, and pure Spirit. . . .*
    . . . Each of these planes corresponds to some part of our spiritual makeup. (pp. 181, 182)

This lesson explores a fascinating person—you. What made you the person you are today? As you come across a phrase or sentence that sheds some light on these causes, you can highlight or underline it.

What's one sentence or phrase in this lesson that especially relates to your life right now?

The Causal Plane (pp. 182–83)

2.   *This plane is the source of* because. (p. 182)

Since this lesson is about asking, do you have a question for the Mahanta, the Living ECK Master? Maybe about something in this discourse that you'd like to explore a little more? Take this opportunity to ask the Inner Master. Open yourself to his response.

Question:

Response:

 This month, you can work with the Mahanta, the Inner Master, on a health condition, a relationship, or a numbing fear. For the special word to chant, see this month's exercise on page 190.

3.   On page 166, your Astral covering was described
      as a starry body. Here's how your Causal body is
      described on page 182.

> *The Causal body is similar to the Astral body*
> *in appearance, but much finer in vibration and*
> *more beautiful. Within it are the impressions of all*
> *previous lives. Also of interest is that the seed for*
> *every condition of your present life was in place*
> *already on the Causal Plane before your birth.*
> (p. 182)

Just for a moment, picture your Causal body. What
does it look like? Feel like? You can describe or
draw it here.

4.   *In fact, karma and reincarnation are much like a mystery story, because many of the events in a person's life weave around motive, means, and opportunity.* (p. 183)

What about your story? What is your motive for this lifetime?

Your means?

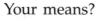

Your opportunity?

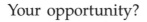

Self-Starter or Victim? (pp. 184–85)

5.   *One group says that a person is largely the cause
of events in life, while the second group feels that
forces beyond the control of an individual are the
prime movers. Of course, these two philosophies are
at odds. Most people, though, fall somewhere between the two extremes, for they feel in control of
certain events, but not of others.* (p. 184)

What's an example of an event in your life where
you feel you are in control, where you are the
cause?

Is there an event in your life that you feel is in the
hands of fate, God, or others? You can jot it here,
if you wish.

Healing the Past (pp. 188–90)

6.   *They usually believe that* others *are the cause of their trouble in the past. Of course, there are lessons to learn from that, too, but those are not in line with the precepts of ECK: acceptance of our total responsibility for every act, condition, or state of mind.* (p. 189)

Reflect for a moment on the benefits of accepting total responsibility for your life. What are the spiritual gifts this could bring? You can list some of the gifts here.

7. As part of this month's spiritual exercise, would
    you like to explore the reason for a certain situa-
    tion in your life? The following quote offers some
    benefits that await you.

>   *That is one of the main benefits of ECK. It can
>   heal all your bodies: the human, the emotional, the
>   causal, and the mental. In the end, you become a
>   spiritual being of love and compassion, with true
>   peace, joy, and contentment.*
>   *You become a cause of life.* (p. 190)

    What condition would you like to offer to the ECK
    for healing? If you wish, you can note it here:

    Health

    Relationship

    Fear

🎧 **Audio Excerpt 11**

A special spiritual exercise is offered in this
excerpt from the talk "Peanut's Hard Road to
Freedom." You're welcome to try it anytime
you feel the need.

This Month's Exercise

A technique to ask the Mahanta for guidance
in your dreams, p. 190

8. Ready to receive a spiritual gift? Try this
    month's spiritual exercise:

    *Briefly, the spiritual exercise this month is
    to chant* Mana *(chanted as mah-NAY). Before
    you begin it, ask the Mahanta about a health
    condition, a relationship, or a numbing fear.
    Then let him guide your dreams, knowing that
    love heals all.* (p. 190)

    Watch your dreams, knowing that love heals
    all. You can record your dreams here or in
    your journal, along with the insights and
    feelings you have when you awaken.

Extra Writing Page
for this month's exercises and experiences

    Your spiritual exercise this month is to practice the art of listening to your loved ones. In addition, sing the holy Sound of God, HU, softly to yourself. (p. 209)

11

Mind Stuff and the Art of Listening

This month let's look at the Mental Plane, where thought, genius, and creation of a material kind abound.

The ECK teachings point to the Mental Plane as the source of philosophy, ethics, and the moral teachings. In addition, this plane is also the home of major religions like Christianity, Hinduism, Buddhism, and many of their offshoots. It is here, then, that they make their heavens.

The Mental Plane is the "third heaven" that Paul speaks of in his second letter to the Corinthians, in chapter 12. Despite this mention in the Bible, it is unlikely that one minister in a hundred has any idea at all what the apostle was talking about. What, then, about the first and second heavens?

Questions about Heaven

An astute researcher would not rest until asking, "Are there heavens beyond the third?" Yet who is there to ask?

Frankly, most people don't lose a lot of sleep over such

fine distinctions as the number of heavens that may exist, because they have their hands full trying to master the art of survival right here. It is mainly the person of a strong religious bent who enters into the full-time service of church or synagogue: minister, priest, rabbi, or other devout figure. Such a person becomes a specialist of sorts in matters of the unseen. The rest of the people look to them for information about heaven and the quality of life there.

Yet the clergy of the Western churches are often like children in their understanding of the other worlds, because their scriptures say little about the many ways a person may enter them. And there is little about people who visit the splendors of heaven every day in this very lifetime, like the ECK Masters. Further, such travelers to the inner worlds—the Far Country—return to everyday life and report their findings to others.

The reason most people have any interest in the invisible worlds at all is due to fear, which religious leaders often excite to keep their followers obedient and docile. It is the basis for the doctrine of hell. A good many hellish places do exist right here on earth, so the clergy have an easy time of it convincing their own to live in a certain way to enjoy a better place in heaven. Yet the other side of the coin is fear. Someone who strays from the fold is in danger of eternal fire, a threat that has served the Christian church for ages. Fear of wolves keeps the flock close.

For example, Matthew 7:15–16 reads: "Beware of false prophets, which come to you in sheep's clothing, but inwardly they are ravening wolves. Ye shall know them by their fruits."

Spiritual Discrimination

A Christian pastor or priest may simply call this good spiritual advice, but at the root of this warning is fear to keep the parishioners meek. Who is to say that a teaching is harmful? "Ye shall know them by their fruits," says Christ in his Sermon on the Mount. This statement is the great qualifier. It shows how to tell whether a person brings truth or falsehood. Yet many people fail to take that extra step of discrimination when first weighing the spiritual teachings of ECK in their minds. If a teaching is new, it must be wrong.

An odd and even humorous point about this view is that people who blast the ideas of other groups are often in the dark about the central beliefs of their own group. Many people who claim to be devout Christians have never read the Bible from cover to cover, even once. They do not know their own scriptures.

Some would laugh at this statement, yet proof lies in the divisions of each major religion. Their followers all profess to believe in the same holy book, but they cannot agree with each other on a common meaning. So they form rival sects and denominations. The many divisions within a mother church are testimony of a deep and serious disagreement among its members about the meaning of their holy scriptures. It could all become a highly volatile issue for a group, and often has.

In the end the question is, Which group within the mother church has the best claim to truth? Attempts to resolve that issue have been the basis for wars and persecution among people of the same church throughout time.

Heavens of Orthodox Religions

So where does the Mental Plane and the so-called higher mind fit into all this?

It is simply that the heavens of the major orthodox

203

religions are still located in the worlds of duality, of good and evil. As said before, the Christian heaven is on the Mental Plane, where something can only exist because of an opposite. Thus, good is the antithesis, or reverse, of evil. The absence of light is darkness. A hill exists only in relation to a plain, a valley, a mountain, or some other object that is unlike itself. A river is not a lake because one is fast and the other is still, or narrow instead of broad.

When a religion's theology and doctrines arise from a plane of duality, as Christianity does from the Mental Plane (the third heaven), then its ideas have a built-in tension. People in that religion will chew upon any differences of belief, even within that group, for time on end, simply because of the nature of the mind.

How Are the Teachings of ECK Different?

In all of the above, I've said very little about the teachings of ECK. How do they differ from the doctrines of other groups?

More than anything, their point of origin is above the Mental Plane. ECKANKAR has many writings about the nature of truth, higher ethics, and social morality—as do other groups—but its viewpoint comes directly from the Light and Sound of God. They are the two pillars of ECK, the Holy Spirit. Divine love is another—and perhaps, better—name for Light and Sound. They fill all space in every world, galaxy, and universe—right up to the highest known kingdom, the Ocean of Love and Mercy. That is the true heaven, the home of God (SUGMAD).

The scriptures of ECK are yours in two ways: (1) through the written and spoken word (the ECK books, talks, and discourses) and (2) through your own direct experience with the Sound and Light (Love) of God.

The purpose of the outer ECK teachings is to lead you to the inner ones, where truth depends upon your own experience of it.

For example, a philosopher or theologian can read and preach about love his entire life and still know nothing about the meaning of love. The main difference between ECKANKAR and many other religions is that ECKANKAR is a teaching of life and love. Christianity, for example, looks to symbols of death, such as the cross, and the virtue of suffering. For much of its history, the Christian church was as much an instrument of censure, torture, and death as it was for peace and love. Especially for those who held to other beliefs.

In fairness, there is a high and a low side to every religion.

All religions have sprung from ECK (the Holy Spirit) in ages past, but rulers, over the centuries, have often swung the pendulum too much toward the pole of power instead of love. The older a religion gets, the more risk there is of its leaders losing touch with the Voice of God, the ECK. It is then that its light grows dim.

It is also then that the ECK Masters of the Vairagi Order bring the original teachings of Light and Sound into the foreground again, to give seekers an exit from the old cycle of karma and rebirth.

Mind Stuff

You can read about the Mental Plane in *ECKANKAR— The Key to Secret Worlds* by Paul Twitchell. There you'll find the traits of a person who falls out of balance with life, and the signs that warn of such a decline in physical, emotional, and mental health. For starters, look in the index under "Mental Plane" and "Mental body." You will find a wealth of information about the inner forces that play with your feelings and judgment, often causing a host of problems to a person who is not aware that such mental facets exist.

Paul Twitchell has covered the structure of the mind and the Mental Plane in the above book as well as in *The Spiritual Notebook* and the two volumes of *The Shariyat-Ki-Sugmad*.

"Mind Stuff and the Art of Listening," the title of this discourse, speaks of two states of being that resist each other. Mind stuff is that which relates to the Mental Plane. It is the whole array of our thoughts and memories, and how they appear in our feelings and actions toward others. The usual problem is that people who are under the influence of this mind stuff are vain and pushy. They like to dominate others by force of will. These people, who need to be in control, are in the habit of meddling with the plans and desires of friends, family, and coworkers. Oddly, they are often miserable and lonely. None will love them.

The Art of Listening

Now, to the art of listening.

Abraham Lincoln, the sixteenth president of the United States, was known for his love and compassion. Friend and foe alike respected him as a good listener, because they knew that whatever the outcome of speaking frankly to him, he would usually act with justice and wisdom.

Three years before becoming president in 1861, Lincoln made an unsuccessful bid for a Senate seat in Illinois. During that campaign, he gave one of his greatest speeches. The country, torn apart by the issue of slavery, was moving rapidly toward civil war when he gave the "House Divided against Itself" speech, in which he clearly and poetically foretold the fate of the United States. It would become either one or the other: all free or all slave.

Before giving that speech, he asked a few close friends to review it. Some of them wanted this sentence removed: "A house divided against itself cannot stand." One said that of course the statement was true, but he doubted whether it was a good idea to address it so directly in those words.

Lincoln listened patiently to all the arguments, then said he'd keep that sentence intact.

"If it must be that I must go down because of this speech," he said, "then let me go down linked to truth, die in the advocacy of what is right and just. This nation cannot live on injustice, 'A house divided against itself cannot stand.' "

And so, we are heirs to one of the greatest speeches of all time. Lincoln listened to others, but he then took their criticisms into his own contemplations, where he weighed the matter by a higher law.

So many people who search for truth are actually in search of love—only they don't know where to find it. Many times they could actually stay with their own religion and find a good measure of happiness and spiritual growth, if they only knew the secret of listening to others with compassion and love. Their hearts would open. In fact, the highest benefit that any spiritual teaching can shower upon its people is to show them the way to divine love. The way to heaven is not through rituals or creeds, because they are food for the mind and offer nothing to Soul, the eternal light of God that you are.

Rebazar Tarzs, the Tibetan ECK Master, says it better in *Stranger by the River*:

"Therefore, if you desire love, try to realize that the

only way to get love is by giving love. That the more you give, the more you get; and the only way in which you can give is to fill yourself with it, until you become a magnet of love."

Listening Is Love

One weekend Joan, my wife, went into a grocery co-op to shop for groceries. A young man in his mid-twenties came into the store and to the aisle where she was selecting produce. The left side of his body seemed to cause him much pain and difficulty; he had a pronounced limp.

Stopping in front of her food cart, he surveyed the items in the bins. "Is the cart in your way?" she asked. "No," he said, "I've never been in here before and was just looking around."

His speech was also strained. Not quite a stutter, it sounded as if his voice has also suffered injury, along with his left arm and leg. Joan simply listened.

From what she could piece together, he had been in a terrible accident that had partially disabled his leg, arm, and also his speech. Yet he seemed grateful for the gift of life.

In him, Joan saw a young man who had recently been on top of the world. Then it caved in on him. Though not very mobile, at least he could walk again. She saw that he desperately needed someone to listen to him, because so many people likely turned away from him as if he were some sort of damaged goods.

Gently she said, "Healing takes time."

He nodded with thanks and understanding; someone had cared enough about him to simply listen. Wishing her a good day, he said, "Take care," and slowly left the store.

This Month's Exercise

Your spiritual exercise this month is to practice the art of listening to your loved ones. In addition, sing the holy Sound of God, *HU*, softly to yourself.

This technique will do more for you than trying to memorize a head full of rules about how to live a better spiritual life.

Listen with love, for the Mahanta is always listening to the whispers of your heart too.

Workbook Activities

1.   *This month let's look at the Mental Plane, where thought, genius, and creation of a material kind abound.*

   The ECK teachings point to the Mental Plane as the source of philosophy, ethics, and the moral teachings. (p. 201)

   Ready for some food for thought?

🎧 Audio Excerpt 12

You can listen to this excerpt from the talk "Recognizing God's Blessings."

This lesson about the Mental Plane offers a feast

of information. What's one point that especially catches your interest? What are you learning about it this month?

To help you live a better spiritual life, try this month's exercise on page 209.

Heavens of Orthodox Religions (pp. 203–4)

2.   *So where does the Mental Plane and the so-called
           higher mind fit into all this?*
              *It is simply that the heavens of the major ortho-
           dox religions are still located in the worlds of dual-
           ity, of good and evil. As said before, the Christian
           heaven is on the Mental Plane, where something can
           only exist because of an opposite. Thus, good is the
           antithesis, or reverse, of evil. The absence of light is
           darkness.* (pp. 203–4)

Heavens that are located in the worlds of duality,
of good and evil, are described on pages 203–4.
Just for a moment, picture a heaven *above* the
Mental Plane—a heaven without an opposite.
What is this like?

3.   *When a religion's theology and doctrines arise from a plane of duality, as Christianity does from the Mental Plane (the third heaven), then its ideas have a built-in tension. People in that religion will chew upon any differences of belief, even within that group, for time on end, simply because of the nature of the mind. (p. 204)*

During the next week, ask the Mahanta to help you notice if you're under the influence of mind stuff and if your mind is chewing on differences. Then sing HU for a moment. You can record some of your experiences or impressions below.

How Are the Teachings of ECK Different? (pp. 204–5)

4. Contemplate on the following words from the
    discourse:

> In all of the above, I've said very little about
> the teachings of ECK. How do they differ from the
> doctrines of other groups?
>
> More than anything, their point of origin is
> above the Mental Plane. . . .
>
> . . . ECKANKAR is a teaching of life and love.
> (pp. 204, 205)

Suppose an interested seeker asks you how the
teachings of ECK are different from orthodox
religions. Speaking from your own experience,
what would you say?

5.   *The scriptures of ECK are yours in two ways: (1) through the written and spoken word (the ECK books, talks, and discourses) and (2) through your own direct experience with the Sound and Light (Love) of God.* (pp. 204–5)

Here's another way to experience the living scriptures of ECK. Open this book at random to any lesson you've read so far. As you glance through it, watch for a phrase or sentence that speaks directly to you. You can put a star by it or jot it here.

6.   *The purpose of the outer ECK teachings is to lead you to the inner ones, where truth depends upon your own experience of it.* (p. 205)

Take a quiet moment to open yourself to the Sound and Light of God, to the divine love that is always here.

For reminders of your inner experiences, you can skim through some of what you've written in this book or in your journal of dreams and insights. You may be pleasantly surprised!

If you wish, you can write a short thank-you note to the Mahanta, the Living ECK Master for these experiences.

The Art of Listening (pp. 206–8)

7.   *Lincoln listened to others, but he then took their criticisms into his own contemplations, where he weighed the matter by a higher law.*

    So many people who search for truth are actually in search of love—only they don't know where to find it. Many times they could actually stay with their own religion and find a good measure of happiness and spiritual growth, if they only knew the secret of listening to others with compassion and love. Their hearts would open. (p. 207)

Add to your study of the importance of listening. You can review Abraham Lincoln's story on pages 206–8.

In the next few days, watch for someone who is a good listener on TV, at work, in class, or at home. What do you observe?

This Month's Exercise

A technique to practice the art of listening
to your loved ones, p. 209

8. You can become a magnet of divine love.
    Ask the Mahanta, the Inner Master, to point
    out opportunities to do the following exercise:

    *Your spiritual exercise this month is to
    practice the art of listening to your loved ones.
    In addition, sing the holy Sound of God, HU,
    softly to yourself. . . .*

    *Listen with love, for the Mahanta is
    always listening to the whispers of your heart
    too.* (p. 209)

    What did you discover? You can record your
    experiences here or in your journal. Use the
    extra writing pages (pp. 218 and 219) if you
    need more space.

Extra Writing Page
for this month's exercises and experiences

Extra Writing Page
for this month's exercises and experiences

Thus, the Mahanta helps quicken your imagination, the means for stirring within you the currents of love, wisdom, and understanding. He shows each person who passes the spiritual tests how to release the far-reaching vision of life, scene by scene. (p. 225)

12

Putting It All Together

After Philip of Macedon had conquered Greece, the King of Sparta sent him this note: "If you measure your shadow, you will find it no greater than before the victory."

Measure your shadow. In the spiritual works, as elsewhere, people try to gauge their success, or that of others, by the standards of outer appearance. It is a temptation to say, "Well, she doesn't act like a Higher Initiate." Or, "If he's so spiritual, why didn't he foresee the problem?" We like to size up people to see whether they stand taller or shorter than us, a way we try to measure our own stature—material or spiritual.

In the end, however, it makes little difference how we stand in relation to anyone or anything but God.

New people in a religion, even on a spiritual path like ECK, like to draw comparisons to what they were and how they felt before coming into it. Some in ECK, aware of very little difference after a year, might say, "What is there in ECK for me?" Others, in an equally shortsighted view of the ways of ECK, will write to the Master in the following manner: "I am far along the spiritual path and want the Fifth Initiation now."

Yet there is also a third group, one that has fewer demands or opinions than the first two. The heart of their communication with the ECK is more likely: "Not my will, but Thine." They let the Mahanta steer them to a richer spiritual life.

Gifts of God

People often accept the gifts of God with less than full appreciation. Much like the squirrels, rabbits, and birds that come to the feeder in my backyard, they expect the feeder of God to fill their hunger.

A few years ago, I used to put out only as much seed as the birds and animals were likely to eat between feedings. They were then quite friendly. Later, however, as I began to set out more seed, in case larger animals like deer dropped by, a strange change occurred in their behavior: The birds and animals became skittish. They lost appreciation for the seed. With the human consciousness, it's often the same way.

The more that people receive from ECK, the less value they give It—unless, of course, the blessings stop. It's human nature. People desire the gifts of God, but otherwise want as little to do with God as possible.

Being Aware or Not

Life is all about being aware or not. Those without an awareness of their place in life are also at the mercy of life, and thus are more likely to be lonely, unhappy, and a victim in every situation that comes along. So the purpose of the ECK teachings is to help all people in ECKANKAR come to a greater awareness of who they are in relation to SUGMAD, the ECK, the Mahanta, and to every other living being. It's a difficult task. It is hard for both the Master and the individual, for it requires effort on both sides. Yet it is the individual who stands to gain the most: divine love and wisdom.

A few days ago, I had a conversation with a young man about a member of the Christian clergy, Jerry, a classmate of mine from many years ago. For sixteen years, Jerry and I had attended the same schools. During grade school, we were usually the only two pupils in our class, because the school was in a small two-roomed building in a farming community. There were fewer than thirty students in the entire school, so Jerry and I naturally were close friends.

Yet we were far different in nature. He was an out-going youth, quick with jokes, good at sports, and at ease in company. Much his opposite, due to the influence of a mother who discouraged the abuse of alcohol and was uncomfortable around the frivolities of dance, I grew up reflective. I felt more at ease in the woods, observing the wonders of nature.

In that way, the first eight of sixteen years passed.

Then we both enrolled at a divinity school, where he and I soon found our own circle of friends. Jerry was a popular student, a part of the in crowd that played sports and made above-average grades. He let others be themselves. My rigid attitudes about religion, on the other hand, became even more so. My friends were students who mostly obeyed the rules, were outcasts, or liked religion class. We allowed too little time for lighthearted fun.

But as I turned twenty, divinity school felt more and more like a closed institution. Two years later, I decided to join the air force. The last time Jerry and I spoke with each other was in early fall of that year, the year he entered a seminary for the final four-year phase of his ministerial studies. Then we lost touch for years. Only recently, he passed his mailing address to a mutual acquaintance, inviting me to write sometime. I wrote a letter to him but haven't received a reply to date.

The youth, with whom I was having this conversation about Jerry, is twenty—nearly the same age as Jerry and me at our last meeting. This young man feels as much uncertainty about his future as we once felt about our own.

So I asked him, "What if Jerry has done a flip-flop? What if he has lost his goodwill and openness toward the beliefs of others since our last meeting? What if he takes this opportunity to try to belittle the works of ECK?"

Jerry used to be open toward the beliefs of others, yet what if he had shut down spiritually and is now more intolerant of others, the way I used to be as a youth about the religious beliefs of others?

I was curious to hear what my young friend would say.

He gave the example of Aaron, who had been a close friend of his from the age of six—as Jerry and I had been. "Aaron liked the in crowd," said my young friend, who himself had enjoyed less popularity than his friend in school. "Aaron always had to keep up appearances, which gave him less freedom than he liked. Still, he let people be themselves. Now that we're out of high school, our friendship is as strong as ever.

"Don't worry about Jerry," the youth said. "He is still the good friend you knew."

What struck me about this young man was his spirit of optimism and goodwill. He gives others a chance, knowing that life furnishes each person with exactly such measure as is in accord with their past deeds. He sees people as spiritual beings, sees strength amid their many failings.

So besides a decline in fear, we also expect to see the qualities of charity and goodwill in those who are further along the path to God.

A Higher State of Consciousness

How does a higher state of consciousness come about? It comes by waking the imagination. The best spiritual teachers, for example, speak in stories and parables, for they know the minds of people are often encased in a hard shell, like that of a walnut. But a story or a parable will break through to the imagination. Intellectuals may scorn this method of conveying a divine message, because a plain story looks far too simple to be effective as an instrument of truth. The imagination, once awakened, is the most dynamic tool in the universe. Like the philosophers' stone, it can change the base metals of human nature into treasures of spiritual gold.

The imagination can open the Spiritual Eye, giving you the ability to see visions, understand dreams, effect healings, attract wealth, and above all, bring greater happiness—on earth and in heaven.

Thus, the Mahanta helps quicken your imagination, the means for stirring within you the currents of love, wisdom, and understanding. He shows each person who passes the spiritual tests how to release the far-reaching vision of life, scene by scene. He reveals but a single precept at a time, for the disciple must first notice it, practice it, discover its limits, and finally, make it his own. Each is a stepping-stone. Each is a step in the direction of God Awareness.

Keys to Heaven

The Sound and Light of ECK are the keys to heaven, and the Mahanta is always ready to help anyone with a desire for truth and love. The Sound and Light are the spiritual food he offers all.

An ECK initiate, on his way to conduct an ECK Worship Service in Mexico City, recently felt the Sound and Light, along with the presence of the Mahanta, the Living ECK Master, while driving there. Soon after leaving home, however, he discovered that he had forgotten some new ECK tapes that he had planned to listen to on the drive. Worse, someone had removed a picture of the Mahanta from his car and had neglected to return it. He wondered what that might mean.

Chanting HU, he tried to understand about the forgotten tapes and the missing photo—when suddenly, he felt the white-gold love of the Mahanta within him. Then he knew with certainty that the Mahanta was guiding his life, even as he was driving his own car.

A waking dream leaped to his attention from a roadside billboard. "Stick to the sound," it read, "and you'll win." It was assurance of the Master's love.

After the ECK Worship Service later that evening, a woman shared the story of how she had found the teachings of ECK a little more than a year earlier. A death had just occurred in the family. In despair and in need of solace, she accepted the invitation of an ECKist to attend an ECK Worship Service, where she found comfort in the HU song. Since then, she had kept coming back. She was grateful for the peace of mind it has slowly brought back into her life.

One day, while singing HU in a Catholic church where she often goes to contemplate, she asked herself what desire she most wanted fulfilled just then. She would ask the ECK for that.

At the time, she was sorely missing her daughter, the family member who had recently met an early death. Her dearest longing was to receive a kiss from her daughter, so she sang HU and asked the ECK to fulfill her wish. Immediately, she felt a warm, loving kiss upon her forehead. Jolted from contemplation, she opened her eyes to find a young boy standing beside her, smiling. He explained she had looked so sad that he only wanted to do something to ease her suffering. But he had nothing to offer, except this kiss.

She hugged and thanked him. She declared that a kiss was precisely what she had been praying for at that moment. Her eyes filled with tears of joy and gratitude, the woman told this story to the ECKists after the ECK Worship Service. Trust had brought her the comfort of a loved one's kiss.

So another sign of spiritual growth is trust in the SUGMAD, the ECK, and the Mahanta.

Embrace the ECK, and Its love will find you.

Imagination

Your watchword now is *imagination*. William Blake, mystic and poet, once said, "The eagle never lost so much time as when he submitted to learn of the crow" ("Proverbs of Hell," *The Marriage of Heaven and Hell*). In the tradition of some Native American tribes, the eagle is a symbol for the spiritual self, while the crow is law, or the mind. The Spiritual Exercises of ECK will link you with the Sound Current (yet another name for the ECK, or Holy Spirit). The Sound Current, of which the holy sound of HU is a part, is the divine melody that can help free your imagination and lift you above the mind, to let you create a new and better spiritual life for yourself.

Here is the sequence of spiritual unfoldment: (1) Have a strong desire for God (as it first expresses itself though a desire for human love, happiness, or fulfillment). (2) Find the Mahanta and the teachings of ECK. (3) Do the spiritual exercises. (4) Let go of fear, so your imagination can take wing through the Spiritual Eye. And finally, (5) accept the higher vision of truth that reveals itself to you.

These are steps on the road to divine love, wisdom, and understanding.

This Month's Exercise

The spiritual exercise for the last discourse in this series is for your protection and comfort as you go about your daily life. The name of this technique is The Invisible Sword.

Whether or not you decide to continue with the outer spiritual instructions of ECK into the coming year, this exercise will always give you an advantage in time of need. It is the dream experience of an ECK initiate who often meets and travels with the Mahanta, the Living ECK Master in the other worlds. We'll call him Mark.

One night, Mark read a passage from *How to Find God*, Mahanta Transcripts, Book 2, on the protection of the Mahanta. Next, he put his attention upon the Light and Sound, and soon rose in consciousness into the higher worlds of Divine Spirit. After the spiritual exercise, he went to bed.

Then he had a vivid dream. He found himself in a medieval setting where the people gave him an invisible sword of impressive weight. When someone attacked him, he had only to hold the sword up and it moved by itself in defense of him. Once, the dreamer misused the sword by wielding it on his own to cut the sword of another knight in half, instead of letting the sword guide and guard him. He realized his error immediately and walked from the fray.

From then on, he carried the invisible sword with him everywhere.

Use the image of the invisible sword whenever you find yourself in distress or trouble, or in need of comfort. Hold it out before you and sing HU, silently or aloud. The sword is the protection of the Mahanta. The strength needed to hold the sword comes from doing the Spiritual Exercises of ECK (like this one).

What are the lessons from Mark's dream?

Trust the protective sword (the Mahanta). Avoid circles where people indulge in power games. And let the sword defend you, for it can help you find spiritual freedom and live beyond the control of others.

This ends a year of study in the works of ECK. I invite you to continue your study of the ECK teachings in the coming year: in your dreams, by Soul Travel, and in your outer studies of the books, recordings, and discourses. Remember to always stay within the heart and love of God.

Despite the title of this series, *The Easy Way Discourses*, the road to God is anything but easy. However, the ECK method is the easiest and most direct of all approaches to SUGMAD, and in the light of that we can indeed say the path of ECK is The Easy Way.

I am always with you.

Harold

⚹

Workbook Activities

1.   *In the end, however, it makes little difference how we stand in relation to anyone or anything but God.* (p. 221)

Picture yourself at home in your favorite room, chatting about this lesson with the Mahanta, the Living ECK Master. As you review your discourse, you can write your comments and questions to the Master here or in the margins of those pages. You can also highlight or underline parts that stand out.

 For protection and comfort, try the Invisible Sword technique, this month's spiritual exercise on pages 228–29.

2.   *Yet there is also a third group, one that has fewer
demands or opinions than the first two. The heart of
their communication with the ECK is more likely:
"Not my will, but Thine." They let the Mahanta
steer them to a richer spiritual life.* (p. 222)

Ask the Mahanta, the Inner Master, to remind you
of a recent situation where you opened yourself to
God's will. Where did it lead you? You can describe your experience here.

Is there something in your life right now that you
would like to turn over to God's will? If so, take a
moment to do this.

231

Gifts of God (p. 222)

3.   *People often accept the gifts of God with less than
full appreciation. . . .*
Life is all about being aware or not. (p. 222)

This exercise can help you to accept the gifts of
God more fully. Visualize yourself surrounded
by a pile of presents—gifts in your life. What are
they? Notice the ones that come to mind right
away.

Then look for gifts you may have taken for
granted, like being able to read, to think, to
breathe.

You can write some of these blessings below.

Look back at the invitation you wrote to the
Master at the beginning of this year (on page 18).
What gift have you received in response to your
note?

Being Aware or Not (pp. 222–25)

4.　　　*What struck me about this young man was his spirit of optimism and goodwill. He gives others a chance, knowing that life furnishes each person with exactly such measure as is in accord with their past deeds. He sees people as spiritual beings, sees strength amid their many failings.*

So besides a decline in fear, we also expect to see the qualities of charity and goodwill in those who are further along the path to God. (p. 224)

Imagine that you're listening to the conversation on pages 223–25. How do these childhood stories relate to you and your life today?

A Higher State of Consciousness (p. 225)

5.   🎧 **Audio Excerpt 13**

Would you like to learn more about the imagination? Listen to this excerpt from the talk "Inside a Circle of Friends."

In the following quote, which gifts of the imagination appeal to you? You can highlight or underline them.

> *How does a higher state of consciousness come about? It comes by waking the imagination. . . .*
> *The imagination can open the Spiritual Eye, giving you the ability to see visions, understand dreams, effect healings, attract wealth, and above all, bring greater happiness—on earth and in heaven.* (p. 225)

You can learn to develop these abilities. Ask the Mahanta, the Inner Master, to show you how the Spiritual Exercises of ECK can free your imagination—and why this is so important. Let your imagination take wing, and open yourself to his response. You can record or sketch your experience here.

✎

Imagination (pp. 227–28)

6.   Let's celebrate your spiritual unfoldment so far! Read the following five steps of spiritual unfoldment, saying them in the first person. For example, "I have a strong desire for God."

> *Here is the sequence of spiritual unfoldment: (1) Have a strong desire for God (as it first expresses itself through a desire for human love, happiness, or fulfillment). (2) Find the Mahanta and the teachings of ECK. (3) Do the spiritual exercises. (4) Let go of fear, so your imagination can take wing through the Spiritual Eye. And finally, (5) accept the higher vision of truth that reveals itself to you.* (pp. 227–28)

This discourse is filled with higher visions of truth along with some stories of people who recognized them. What about your story? Take a quiet moment to remember a time when the ECK teachings came alive for you. You can record your experience below, if you wish.

✍

This Month's Exercise

The Invisible Sword technique for protection and comfort, pp. 228–29

7.   *The spiritual exercise for the last discourse in this series is for your protection and comfort as you go about your daily life. The name of this technique is The Invisible Sword.* (p. 228)

As you read "This Month's Exercise," on pages 228–29, you can draw a star by the tips that may help your inner journeys. Or you can jot them below.

Look for hints on how to travel with the Mahanta.

Spotlight on ECK:
Noticing and Remembering the Spiritual Gifts

8.   *Use the image of the invisible sword whenever you find yourself in distress or trouble, or in need of comfort. Hold it out before you and sing HU, silently or aloud. The sword is the protection of the Mahanta. The strength needed to hold the sword comes from doing the Spiritual Exercises of ECK (like this one). (p. 229)*

If you wish, ask the Mahanta, the Inner Master, to remind you about this invisible sword whenever the need arises in the future. Listen for his whisper.

You can record any experiences here, in your journal, or on the extra writing page (p. 238). These entries will bear witness to your growing spiritual strength and connection with the Mahanta.

Extra Writing Page
for this month's exercises and experiences

What's Next?

Dear Friend:

You have just completed a year of ECK study and are now ready for the next discourse series, *The ECK Dream 1 Discourses*.

You will find the study of dreams in ECK unique. It is to make you aware of all that you ever were, are, or could hope to be in this lifetime.

Dream study is still in its infancy, in spite of Freud, Jung, and others. The problem is, no one can corral dreams with symbols or logic. Our dream worlds are real, but in their own way, and the mind can only measure the smallest bit of them.

So, then, how do the ECK Masters regard dreams? They say that you are Soul, a light of God born into this world for spiritual experience. They also teach that you and I are individuals with a past—a long past. Within each of us is the memory of who and what we have ever been. The purpose of dream study in ECK is to find out who we are. Then, and only then, can we develop into spiritual giants, like the ECK Masters.

In this study of dreams, you will sooner or later meet a very important teacher—the Dream Master. He is the ECK Adept who comes into your dreams.

The purpose of *The ECK Dream 1 Discourses* is to open you to your own inner guidance. The Dream Master will bring you a different kind of dream than you have ever known and can help you understand what before were only jumbled dreams of little value. In time, he will replace them with dreams of insight, wisdom, and knowledge. They are about the most important person in the world—you.

The ECK Dream 1 Discourses are an outer study. They enable you to meet the Dream Master, who simply wants to see you gain the attributes of God: wisdom, power, and freedom. But more, he knows that on your journey to God you will also find the most important thing of all—love. He is your protector. He is also a teacher, guide, and friend, and becomes a part of your secret life.

This twelve-month series includes these titles: "Dreams—The Bridge to Heaven," "The Dream Master," "How to Interpret Your Dreams," "Dream Travel to Soul Travel," and more.

The ECK Dream 1 Discourses are the next step in your personal spiritual training in ECKANKAR.

With spiritual blessings,

Harold Klemp

Workbook Activities

1. *The purpose of dream study in ECK is to find out who we are. Then, and only then, can we develop into spiritual giants, like the ECK Masters.* (p. 239)

    Here's a preview of the next year of spiritual study. As you read the invitation from the Mahanta, the Living ECK Master on pages 239–40, what parts inspire you to become a greater spiritual being?

2. The following quote gives a peek into the world that awaits you.

> *You will find the study of dreams in ECK unique. It is to make you aware of all that you ever were, are, or could hope to be in this lifetime. . . .*
>
> *The purpose of* The ECK Dream 1 Discourses *is to open you to your own inner guidance. The Dream Master will bring you a different kind of dream than you have ever known and can help you understand what before were only jumbled dreams of little value. In time, he will replace them with dreams of insight, wisdom, and knowledge. They are about the most important person in the world—you.* (pp. 239–40)

🎧 Audio Excerpt 14

You can hear how a dream inspired a woman to create a better life for herself in this excerpt from the talk "The Dream Master, Part 2."

Now take a few moments for a little daydream. Imagine how it would feel to fully enjoy and understand your dream worlds every night. What would your waking life be like?

Draw a cartoon or sketch of something from your daydream, for your eyes only. You can also add a comment about how you feel.

✎

3.   The ECK Dream 1 Discourses *are an outer study. They enable you to meet the Dream Master, who simply wants to see you gain the attributes of God: wisdom, power, and freedom. But more, he knows that on your journey to God you will also find the most important thing of all—love. He is your protector. He is also a teacher, guide, and friend, and becomes a part of your secret life.* (p. 240)

Would you like to remember more of your ongoing meetings with the Mahanta, the Living ECK Master? He appears in your dreams as the Dream Master.

You can write a note below, asking for any—or all—of the help he offers to you.

Spotlight on ECK:
Noticing and Remembering the Spiritual Gifts

4.   *You are Soul, a light of God born into this world for spiritual experience.* (p. 239)

Each day, as you prepare to do your contemplation, you can ask the Mahanta, the Inner Master, what exercise to do.

If you wish, turn to the table of contents, pages iii–v. It gives short descriptions of the different exercises you were given throughout the past year. You're always welcome to do any of these at any time. Perhaps one will light up for you to try.

You may want to note below which exercises you did, along with anything you perceived. Your journal entries can serve as a record of the spiritual experiences that you, a light of God, are constantly having.

RECORDINGS
AND
MAHANTA TRANSCRIPTS

If you enjoy the audio excerpts that come with this discourse, you may be interested in more complete versions of these talks. They are available as recordings and as chapters in the Mahanta Transcripts series of books from ECKANKAR, PO Box 2000, Chanhassen, MN 55317-2000 USA. Tel (952) 380-2222, Fax (952) 380-2196, www.Eckankar.org. Item numbers (e.g., #101691) are included below for your convenience.

Excerpt 1: "The Right of Choice," from *Sunshine and Sparkle/The Right of Choice/A Larger Room*, 1994 ECK Worldwide Seminar, audiocassette #101691
Chapter 2 of *The Secret of Love*, Mahanta Transcripts, Book 14, #011333

Excerpt 2: *True Wisdom*, 2003 ECK Spiritual Skills Seminar, audiocassette #102031, DVD #202262

Excerpt 3: "Just for Love," from *Just for Love/Our Spiritual Wake-Up Calls/A Servant of God*, 1996 ECK Springtime Seminar, audiocassette #101751
Just for Love, DVD #201922
Chapter 5 of *Our Spiritual Wake-Up Calls*, Mahanta Transcripts, Book 15, #011343

Excerpt 4: "The Dream Master, Part 1," from *The Dream Master*, Parts 1 and 2, 1988 ECK Worldwide Seminar, audiocassette #101321

Chapter 1 of *The Dream Master*, Mahanta Transcripts, Book 8, #011273

Excerpt 5: *The Law of Returns*, 2004 ECK Spiritual Skills Seminar, audiocassette #102051, DVD #202282

Excerpt 6: *God's Love Is a Wonderful Thing*, 1999 ECK Springtime Seminar, audiocassette #101881, DVD #202122
Chapter 12 of *How to Survive Spiritually in Our Times*, Mahanta Transcripts, Book 16, #011353

Excerpt 7: *The Rope of Karma*, 1984 Regional Seminar, CD #101243
Chapter 5 of *The Golden Heart*, Mahanta Transcripts, Book 4, #011233

Excerpt 8: "Walk with Me, Mahanta," from *Welcome Home to the Teachings of ECK/Walk with Me, Mahanta/Five Spiritual Laws of This World*, 1995 ECK Springtime Seminar, audiocassette #101701
Chapter 6 of *The Secret of Love*, Mahanta Transcripts, Book 14, #011333

Excerpt 9: *The Secret of Love*, Temple of ECK Worship Service, August 6, 1995, audiocassette #101731
Chapter 10 of *The Secret of Love*, Mahanta Transcripts, Book 14, #011333

Excerpt 10: "God Is Speaking through You," from *God Is Speaking through You/The Meaning of Surrender/Protection of the Master*, 1987

ECK Creative Arts Festival, audiocassette #101251
Chapter 11 of *Unlocking the Puzzle Box*, Mahanta Transcripts, Book 6, #011253

Excerpt 11: "Peanut's Hard Road to Freedom," from *The Way to Spiritual Freedom/Peanut's Hard Road to Freedom*, 1992 ECK Summer Festival, audiocassette #101561
Chapter 11 of *What Is Spiritual Freedom?* Mahanta Transcripts, Book 11, #011303

Excerpt 12: *Recognizing God's Blessings*, Temple of ECK Worship Service, February 6, 1994, audiocassette #101671
Chapter 7 of *The Slow Burning Love of God*, Mahanta Transcripts, Book 13, #011323

Excerpt 13: *Inside a Circle of Friends*, 1999 ECK Summer Festival, audiocassette #101891, DVD #202132
Chapter 13 of *How to Survive Spiritually in Our Times*, Mahanta Transcripts, Book 16, #011353

Excerpt 14: "The Dream Master, Part 2," from *The Dream Master*, Parts 1 and 2, 1988 ECK Worldwide Seminar, audiocassette #101321
Chapter 2 of *The Dream Master*, Mahanta Transcripts, Book 8, #011273